If You Can Walk, You Can Dance

If You Can Talk, You Can Sing

If You Can Walk, You Can Dance

If You Can Talk, You Can Sing

A Successful African-American

Doctoral Fellowship Program

S. David Stamps & Israel Tribble Jr.

Beckham House Publishers, Inc.
Silver Spring, MD 20907

Dr. S. David Stamps is a Professor of Sociology at the
University of South Florida, Tampa.

Dr. Israel J. Tribble, Jr. is President of the Florida
Education Fund, Tampa, Florida.

Published in the United States by
Beckham House Publishers, Inc.
P.O. Box 8008, Silver Spring, MD 20907
ISBN: 0-931761-44-1 paper
0-931761-43-3 cloth

10987654321

Contents

List of Tables

Acknowledgments

I want to especially acknowledge the work of Dr. David Stamps, Principal Investigator and Dr. Diane Briscoe, Coordinator of this study. Both have been tireless workers and prolific conceptualizers, researchers and writers. I would like to specifically point to the second chapter, which was completed by Dr. Brisco, for its breadth, thoroughness and usefulness. This is a very important baseline for the entire study in terms of placing the McKnight Doctoral Fellowship Program in the context of previous research. This also adds a tremendous amount of credence to all that has been accomplished and that which is yet to be accomplished.

It is also important for me to recognize Mr. Henry Drury, Program Officer at the Mellon Foundation who had the confidence in the Florida Education Fund and its McKnight Doctoral Fellowship Program to place funding at our disposal. This support has allowed us to very systematically look at what it is that we have accomplished and how the Fellows are responding to our overall efforts, as well as to compare their performance and perceptions with those of a significant group of African-American doctoral students throughout the state of Florida. Without his support and interest, we would not have been able to provide this seminal piece of scholarship for the higher education community.

I also want to thank Ms. Joycelyn Reed, Mr. Wuan Head, LTC (R) Ron Nelson, and Mrs. Donna Floyd for their steadfastness and their valuable contribution to this manuscript. Without their individual and collective participation, we would not have been able to arrive at such a high quality effort represented by this study. It is our desire that this study be shared with a very broad range of faculty, students, policy makers and institutions so that we may truly influence not only the production, but also the quality of the graduate education experience for all those who would strive to complete the requirements for the doctoral degree.

Israel Tribble Jr.
President
Florida Education Fund

1

Objectives of the Evaluative Study

When Europeans first came to these shores, the continent was immediately beset with demographic challenges. The sharing of wealth, the distribution of land, and contact with, or control of, the native population ensured such challenges. After the birth of the nation, wave after wave of immigrants flowed across the Atlantic, and later the Pacific, seeking a better life. The tired, the poor and often the uneducated came and kept coming. This continuous influx of different people, bringing both brawn and brain, helped to shape and mold the developing nation. As it turned out, the diversity of population became the nation's greatest asset.

But the history of higher education in this country shows a continued opposition to accepting diversity as a real strength. Universities were designed for, and populated by, White men—a select group of White men. Joseph Gusfield points out in *Campus Power Struggle* (Trans-action, 1970) that although egalitarian values always stressed mass education, in practice only those persons labeled academically talented as measured by scores and grades, and those from well-off families were recruited. This status quo maintained itself until after World War II when the demographic challenge of post-World War II baby boomers obliged educators, politicians and the federal government to respond. Old facilities were updated; new colleges and universities built, and a system of community colleges developed. More schools meant more students and a competition ensued for these undergraduates.

Aided by a postwar economic boom that made scholarships and other sources of financing available, African Americans, veterans, women and working-class youths began to matriculate at these schools in greater numbers (Skolnick, 1969). The change in the numbers and in the kinds of students recruited, and in many cases even the kind of faculty, broke down the traditional relationship that had existed between students and administrators since the 19th century (see Becker, 1970 and Horowitz, 1986).

Veterans entering college in the late 1950s were a prime mover in this new order. Generally, they were older than their counterparts, had fought for their country and did not readily accept the rules of governance tolerated by students before them.

At varying times, joining veterans on campus were African Americans and women. African Americans came to campus during the 1960s buoyed by events in Africa as the colonial system was breaking down and by the increasing civil disobedience displayed by African Americans in the South. These students came to campus prepared not to accept what they viewed as unfair treatment and racist attitudes (Skolnick, 1969).

Women arrived on campus unwilling to accept their traditional roles that carried the expectation that college women consort with college men, join sororities, win honor by appearance and style and not seriously compete academically (Horowitz, 1986).

Even the traditional college student came to campus more "morally and politically serious and better educated than the generation of the 1950s" (Skolnick, 1969).

During the 1970s, both inflation and recession threatened the national prosperity. This economic downturn naturally a higher education. Young adults who were enjoying economic and career successes now felt that their own positions were threatened. They became less concerned with giving a helping hand to others. As the economic pie became smaller, they perceived it impossible to maintain their prosperous lifestyle and at the same time support programs for the poor and disadvantaged minorities. Something had to give and it wasn't going to be their advantageous lifestyle. The "me generation" was born.

In the late 1970s and throughout most of the 1980s, this wave of conservatism perceptibly influenced the attitudes of college and university administrators in their responses to minority students.

The demographic and social changes affecting higher education during the 1960s, 1970s and part of the 1980s set the stage for the issues and trends we face today in higher education. Wilson and Justiz (1987-88) maintain that the "demographic [challenges of the past] are relatively minuscule compared to what lies ahead."

As the 21st Century approaches, demographic predictions by Hodgkinson (1985) were factors that prodded American educators to re-evaluate the current directions of American education and to establish new priorities (Borkowski, 1988). Given (1) the history of challenges that faced higher education just sketched, (2) the aftermath of the Civil Rights Movement and (3) the promise of President Johnson's "Great Society," one would have thought that by 1990 the African-American participation rate in education—from kindergarten through the doctoral degree—would have increased significantly.

Further, one would have expected a similar increase with teachers and administrators throughout the education system. However, despite increases in participation and graduation rates in higher education until the mid-1970s, just the opposite is occurring.

In its *Eight Annual Status Report* (Carter and Wilson, 1980) the American Council on Education revealed some startling statistics about the educational status of African Americans. Of all racial/ethnic groups, African Americans had the most significant drop in degrees conferred. This decrease was due, in part, to a significant drop in college participation rates among African-American males. Between 1976 and 1988, the college participation rate for 18 to 24 year-old African-American high school graduates dropped from 40 percent to 30 percent (Carter and Wilson). Most alarming was the fact that middle-income African Americans showed the most dramatic decreases in college participation rates, dropping from 53 percent in 1976 to 36 percent in 1988. The most severe decreases occurred among middle-income African-American males. For 1987, 9.2 percent of undergraduates nationally were African Americans. Yet, they accounted for only 5.7 percent of the baccalaureate degrees awarded. Gender differences in degrees awarded to African Americans also existed. African-American males had the most dramatic decreases in baccalaureate degrees between 1976 and 1985. This trend continued until 1987, but decreases were not as dramatic as those through 1985.

When college participation rates for African Americans are viewed in terms of demographic projections, the challenge facing higher education should become a national priority. These projections indicate that the minority college-age population will decline significantly over the next two decades. Given the higher birth rates and continuing rates of immigration, minorities (especially African Americans and Hispanics) will make up 30 percent of the population (Hodgkinson, 1985). By the year 2050, the U.S. population could increase from 255 million in 1992 to 385 in 2050. Forty-seven percent of the population is projected to be minorities (*Business Week*, 1992:29). These demographic changes will affect both the American economic system and the American education system by tipping the delicate balance that exists between work force needs and the availability of workers with the necessary education and technical skills. Important also will be the decline in the number of available traditional entry-level workers and the increase in the median age of White Americans (State Higher Education Executive Officers, 1987).

For African Americans, a decline in the pool of White entry-level workers will provide an excellent opportunity for economic advancement. However, there are now trends in education that will compromise that opportunity. These trends include: (1) the quality of education provided to minorities in kindergarten through grade 12; (2)

inaccessibility to higher education, especially graduate education, and (3) the disproportionately low number of African-American faculty in higher education.

The quality of education from kindergarten through the 12th grade has been discussed extensively in educational literature. The listing that follows is an example: Boyer, 1983; Carnegie Corporation, 1983; National Commission on Excellence Reform, 1983; Hodgkinson, 1985; The College Board, 1985, and Quality Education for Minorities Project, 1990.

Data have already been presented in this study showing "pipeline" problems that exist for African Americans at the undergraduate level. Of course, the pipeline problems at any level below that exacerbates the problem.

Since the focus of this study is on African- American doctoral students, our emphasis is placed on graduate education and college and university faculties of the future. So far, we have shown that over the last decade, higher education has not responded to the higher graduation rates among African-American high school students. In fact, the college participation rate of African-American high school graduates has declined. Since the mid-1970s, there has been a lack of progress in making higher education accessible or desirable to African Americans. It stands to reason that, in general, if undergraduate participation declines, the participation rate will also decease at the graduate level. Carter and Wilson (1989) observed that from 1976 to 1987 there was a decrease (31.8 percent) in the number of Master's degrees awarded to African Americans. For African-American males there was a 34 percent decrease in Master's degrees. From 1978 to 1988 there was a 22.1 percent decrease in the doctoral degrees awarded African Americans, with a 46.7 percent decrease among African-American males.

Table 1 in this study supports the Carter and Wilson findings. Comparing African Americans who earned doctorates with other racial/ethnic groups, from 1980 through 1991 the percentage of total doctorates received increased for all groups except Blacks. In 1980 there were 1,032 doctorates awarded to Blacks. By 1991, this number had decreased to 9,933, or 3.8 percent of the total. In 1977, 1,116

African Americans received doctorates, an all time high according to Wycliff (1990) after studying figures form the National Research Council. If this seems discouraging, in some other academic fields it is even worse.

Table 1:
Total doctorates earned by U.S. citizens by race and ethnicity: 1980-91

Year	1980	1981	1982	1983	1984	1985	1986	1987	1988	1989	1990	1991
Total U.S. Citizens	25,221	25,061	24,388	24,358	24,026	23,363	23,081	22,991	23,172	28,172	24,190	24,721
Native American	75	85	77	81	74	95	99	115	93	93	94	130
% of Total	0.30%	0.30%	0.30%	0.30%	0.30%	0.40%	0.40%	0.50%	0.40%	0.40%	0.40%	0.52%
Asian	458	465	452	492	512	516	531	542	612	624	617	762
% of Total	1.80%	1.90%	1.90%	2.00%	2.10%	2.20%	2.30%	2.40%	2.60%	2.70%	2.55%	3.08%
African - American	1,032	1,013	1,047	922	953	912	823	767	805	811	828	933
% of Total	4.10%	4.00%	4.30%	3.80%	4.00%	3.90%	3.60%	3.30%	3.50%	3.50%	3.42%	3.80%
Hispanic	412	464	535	539	536	561	572	619	594	570	700	710
% of Total	1.60%	1.90%	2.20%	2.20%	2.20%	2.40%	2.50%	2.70%	2.60%	2.45%	2.90%	2.90%
White	21,993	21,980	21,677	21,699	21,349	20,757	20,626	20,470	20,685	20,688	21,650	21,859
% of Total	87.20%	87.70%	88.90%	89.10%	88.90%	88.80%	89.40%	89.00%	89.30%	89.30%	89.50%	88.42%
Unknown	1,251	1,054	600	625	602	522	430	478	383	387	304	331
% of Total	5.00%	4.20%	2.50%	2.60%	2.50%	2.20%	1.90%	2.10%	1.70%	1.70%	1.25%	1.33%

Source: National research Council, Summary Report 1988, Statistical Profile of Doctorate Recipients by Race/Ethnicity and Citezenship, 1989, 1990, 1991, pps. 15, 68-9,70-1,76-7

Table 2 shows that of the 9,600 doctorates awarded in the natural sciences and engineering in 1989, only 133 or 1.39 percent were awarded to African Americans. Wycliff (1990) further states that the 133 degrees awarded African Americans in 1989 represents a 12 percent increase over the 124 awarded in 1988. In actuality, the 133 doctorates awarded African Americans in 1989 matched the highest number ever received in the natural sciences and engineering, which was in 1978. Efforts to increase the number of doctorates awarded African Americans have been the concern of educators for the past two decades. However, the annual production rate has remained between 100 and 133 during that period (Wycliff, 1990).

Table 2:
Doctorates awarded African Americans in natural sciences and engineering: 1989

Academic Field	Number of Degrees	Percent of Total Awareded
Life Sciences	75	*1.66%*
Biology	44	1.42%
Health Sciences	24	3.32%
Agriculture	7	1.02%
Physical Sciences	*35*	*1.09%*
Physics/Astronomy	5	0.74%
Chemistry	20	1.55%
Earth, Marine and Atmospheric Sciences	3	0.57%
Mathematics	6	1.53%
Computer Sciences	1	0.30%
Engineering	*23*	*1.24%*
Total	***133***	***1.39%***

Source: National Research Council. Taken from Don Wycliff, "Blacks' Advance Slow in Science Careers," *The New York Times* (June 8, 1990) : pp. A1 and A9.

For this study, the decline in undergraduate and particularly graduate school participation rates for African Americans underlines the crux of the problems to be addressed. At a time when African Americans have an opportunity to enter graduate school and to make a career in higher education, their rates of participation at both the undergraduate and graduate levels are declining and will impact an already limited supply in the African-American faculty pool.

Higher education is facing the prospect of a significant decrease in the availability of a pool of faculty to draw from as these current demographic changes take place. Further exacerbating the situation is the prediction that by the year 2000 approximately 50 percent of the current faculty will retire (Wilson and Justiz, 1987-88). It has been estimated that over the next 25 years between 150,000 and 650,000 faculty positions will be available (Office of Graduate Studies, 1989). Bowen and Schuster (1986) are more specific in that they predict that between 1985 and 2009 approximately 67 percent of the American faculty in 1985 will be replaced. An acute shortage of faculty in certain areas, most notable business, has already occurred. The result is that faculty salaries in fields such as accounting, finance, management and marketing have escalated significantly. Given these predicted shortages of faculty, coupled with the changing demographics, African-American faculty will be increasingly sought for faculty positions. Unless significant changes occur, a seemingly bright employment picture in higher education for African Americans will, in fact, not be realized. Current data reveal an already vast under-representation of Black faculty on college and university faculties nationwide. Blackwell (1984) and Harvey (1986) estimate that African Americans constitute only 4.2 percent of all college and university faculty members, a decease from a late 1970s estimate of approximately 6 percent. Even 4.2 percent is deceiving when one factors out African-American faculty at predominantly Black colleges and universities. These statistics reveal why the competition for African-American faculty has escalated to the present levels; there are currently not enough to go around. But more important, there are too few in the graduate school pipeline.

In higher education the under-representation of minorities is further exacerbated by an uneven distribution of doctorates. According to Blackwell (1984), approximately 50 percent of all doctorates granted annually to African Americans are in education. After education, African Americans are likely to pursue degrees in the social sciences.

Demographic changes are under way that will create the need for a better educated and a more highly skilled minority workforce, that is, if American society is to remain economically competitive. However, at a time when these human resource needs are rising, education pipeline problems have increased for minorities, especially African Americans. In keeping with the focus of this report, pipeline problems seem most acute at the graduate level. Therefore it is most appropriate that an evaluative study be conducted of the McKnight Black Doctoral Program. Since its inception in 1984, the McKnight Program has gained national attention for its recruitment, retention and graduation of African-American doctoral students in degree programs other than in the field of education.

Objectives of the Evaluative Study

For the most part, higher education has been non responsive to the education of African Americans. The exception was the era of the Civil Rights Movement (1955-1976) when the participation rate for African Americans reached an all-time high (Wilson and Justiz, 1987-88). Since 1976-77, African-American participation rates in higher education have been in decline, including those at the doctoral level. Although slight gains have been made over the last few years at the doctoral level, these increases have only had the effect of slowing the rate of decrease (Carter and Wilson, 1989). However, as the American society moves toward the 21st Century, there are compelling reasons for higher education to reverse its *laissez-faire* posture of the late 1970s and most of the 1980s. It has been acknowledged that the level of quality provided African-American students in kindergarten through high school and problems associated with accessibility and retention at the undergraduate level cannot be overlooked as having an impact on graduate education. However, while this impact needs to be addressed, it is beyond the scope of this evaluative study.

The focus of this study is on African-American participation at the doctoral level. The question can be raised: What are the salient facts that influence the success of African-American doctoral students? More specific, the primary objective of this study is to compare African-American students attending Florida doctoral granting universities in the McKnight Black Doctoral Program with those who were not. It was expected that significant differences existed between the two groups (McKnight vs. non-McKnight) on many of the variables that have been shown in the literature as being important in recruitment and retention to graduation (see Blackwell, 1983, 1987; 1988; Avakian, 1982; Busch, 1985; McKenna and Lewis, 1986; Pruitt and Issac, 1985; Richardson and Gerlach, 1980). These variables include:

I. Educational background
- type of college attended
- graduate degree holder
- undergraduate discipline
- graduate discipline
- educational background of parent/guardian

II. Support mechanisms
- financial support
- opportunities for professional growth and development
- mentoring
- networking
- bonding
- role models
- institutional support system
- influences to attend graduate school

III. Personal qualities/achievement
- leader as undergraduate
- grade point average

2

Recruitment and Retention in Traditional Institutions:

Issues Relating to Minority Graduate School Success

There is no discernible disagreement in the literature on the need for more minority recruitment and retention in higher education. The need for colleges and universities to seek strategies to ensure the success of minority graduate students is an issue that most institutions are willing to support. What is more elusive, however, are the desired outcomes: increased minority enrollments, reduction in the levels of attrition by minorities, and increased graduation rates at the graduate and professional school levels for minority students.

The purposes of this section of the study are: 1) to review current literature to ascertain the criteria being used by graduate and professional schools, and 2) to determine the criteria that are endorsed by researchers to enhance the graduation rates of minority students in post-secondary institutions, specifically at the doctoral level.

Background

Previously, issues related to the educational experiences of minorities tended to focus on elementary and secondary school. The increase in the numbers of African Americans attending mainstream institutions of higher education has widened that focus to include postsecondary education (Allen, 1982). The areas receiving intense scrutiny have generally been recruitment and retention. It is difficult to discuss one without the other; the two seem inextricably interwoven.

Research on the experiences of graduate students at the doctoral and professional school levels is scarce (Allen, 1982, 1984; Clewell, 1987). There are many difficulties associated with collecting data on minority participation, perceptions and performance in graduate education. Among the difficulties is the absence of a universally accepted definition of the term "minority" (Issac, 1986). Another is the severe underrepresentation of minority graduate students at the doctoral level, particularly African Americans (Nettles, 1990; VANT and Assoc., 1988; Clewell, 1987; Kolbert, 1989; Adams, 1988; Chandler, 1988; Marks, 1984; Owens, 1976; Isaac, 1986). It is often impossible to conduct research on issues related to African-American graduate students due to their small numbers. In a study for the Educational Testing Service, Clewell (1987) found sample size at the doctoral level to be particularly problematic.

Most of the available research in the areas of minority recruitment and retention can be classified into one of two categories. The first is an analysis of existing data: student demographic and status data such as enrollment characteristics and academic standing at the time of admission. The second is an analysis of student perceptions. The latter would be most beneficial, but is least available. Exploring student perceptions can provide insight directly into the issues that relate to their success (Clewell, 1987).

As indicated in chapter one, changing demographics have exacerbated the need for additional data on graduate level study. Most demographers project that by the year 2,000, 30 percent of the U.S. population will be nonwhite. Many officials in higher education understand these projected changes and have discussed ways to improve minority enrollments, particularly at the graduate level. The fact remains, however, that despite their expressed efforts, little real change has occurred: minority enrollments at the graduate level are proportionately minuscule, and recruitment and retention issues remain high on the stated priority lists of most college and university administrators.

In particular, African-American students are acutely underrepresented in doctoral programs across the United States. Thomas (1987) found support for earlier studies that indicated a decreasing proportion of African-American doctoral and professional students in the pipeline (Chapter 1 of this study provided indepth productivity data with regard to African-American doctoral students.)

Recruitment and Retention
Review of Related Research

Most of the doctoral degrees earned by African-American students have been awarded in the field of education. The enrollment of doctoral students in the natural and hard sciences is negligible, (Adams, 1988; Boyd, 1977; Mommsen, 1974; Thomas, 1987). Furthermore, severe shortages are projected in critical professional areas such as medicine, law, computer science, business, humanities and the social sciences (Blackwell, 1981).

In an effort to remedy this situation, many colleges and universities have attempted to improve recruitment and retention efforts. These institutions have identified what they perceived to be key factors in successful recruiting. These factors have included improved advising, increased financial assistance, improved faculty sensitivity to minority needs, the presence of minority faculty as role models and mentors, and enhanced student support systems. Yet, most of these are factors with which minority students have expressed dissatisfaction: lack of access and advising, inaccessibility to, and insensitivity of, faculty, inadequate financial assistance, and lack of opportunities for counseling services (Allen, 1982; Clewell, 1987). Research findings based on student-reported data suggest that university responsiveness and performance in these areas have been less than effective (Allen, 1984). This leads one to conclude that if the factors critical to recruitment and retention have been correctly identified by institutions, then the process used to ensure their successful implementation has been flawed.

Trent and Copeland (1988) looked at the decrease in graduate school participation among African-American students from 1972 to 1974 and found unequal emphasis on recruitment and retention. The support provided during the first year of graduate study and the weakening support offered in subsequent years tended to favor recruitment over retention efforts.

Willie, et. al. (1991) provided additional strength to these findings. They observed that African-American doctoral students often fail to complete their degrees because of the lack of financial assistance in their later years of study.

When recruitment and retention efforts have met with limited success, the rationale frequently offered by institutions for the lack of improvement has most often included: a scarce applicant pool; an inability to locate students willing to attend; the "raiding" of talented students by business and industry; an inability of the identified students to meet university standards; an inability of students to meet university graduate school admissions requirements; lack of institutional resources to provide adequate financial aid, and a lack of minority faculty role models (Kolbert, 1989; Boyd, 1977; VANT, 1988; Wilson and Justiz, 1987).

Institutional Factors Hindering Success

In reality, other pertinent issues are often overlooked. Many of these issues are related to communication barriers (Allen, 1984), human factors and the environment within the institutions to which these minority students are recruited. These circumstances mitigate against significant gains in the areas of recruitment and retention.

More specific, in principle many institutions are committed to the inclusion of diverse populations at all levels of the university structure. However, institutions do not implement policy, *people* do.

Universities are a microcosm of society. Policies related to diversity may run counter to the philosophies held by many of the personnel entrusted with implementing the universities' policies.

The lack of commitment to diversity at the department level may also be a factor. The importance of academic departments to the process cannot be overstated. It is also at this level that most faculty and students interact. It is also the level at which criteria are established for program admissions and assistantships are awarded (Adams, 1986; Isaac, 1986; Allen, 1984).

The negative reactions of faculty and staff to institutional efforts toward inclusion (reactions against what may be perceived as "political correctness") may also hinder efforts toward the implementation of strategies identified as important to success. Astin's (1982) research on the Bakke and Defunis court cases shows that these decisions have resulted in increased resistance to special admissions and affirmative action policies.

Although institutional policies may express exemplary goals, the hostile reaction of many functionaries preclude full implementation. The perception among many of these institutional representatives is that too much is already being done to assist minority students. Given this attitude of resistance, Astin (1982) finds that individuals in authority in institutions often serve as "gatekeepers"—institutional representatives who control and limit entry into prestige positions. Allen's (1984) findings suggest that the experiences of African-American students in higher education are less than ideal. Social adjustment, student interactions with faculty, and campus race relations are issues deserving continued scrutiny. Students in Allen's study characterized their interactions with faculty as "ambivalent" or "negative". The importance of assessing faculty and departmental attitudes, and of developing a sensitivity to racial attitudes cannot be overemphasized (Fang, 1987).

Success at the doctoral level is largely a subjective process and requires that students be integrally involved with faculty committees. The unique operating style purported to be characteristic of many faculty, and the inability or unwillingness of many mainstream faculty to fully understand the issues faced by minority students on their campuses may be inhibiting. Even when students are able to meet the *formal* requirements of their programs, they may not have the wherewithal to "fully integrate themselves into the informal networks of the institutional system" (Allen, 1984, p. 9). According to Abatso (1987), students who have control of their destiny are more successful and are better able to identify financial support. African-American students are seldom in a position to control their destiny.

"The issue is not whether Blacks are desirous of education, but whether circumstances allow a quality education even when they want one," according to Dr. Israel Tribble (Ryan, 1989, p. 1).

Student Perceptions of Factors Hindering Success

Students reported in the research of Clewell (1987) and Nettles (1990) that key institutional elements in preventing success included a hostile educational and racial environment, ineffective advising, an unsupportive dissertation committee, lack of social interaction, lack of interaction with faculty, lack of a supportive mentor, and financial hardship. Many of these are circumstances over which institutions and departments have direct control. Allen (1982) found that the African-American students in his study perceived subtle expectations of failure and experienced marginal social interaction with mainstream faculty. Many African-American students endure social isolation on campus (Carrington and Sedlacek, 1976; Allen, 1982), and feel alienated (Nettles, 1990; Allen, 1984). They further perceive an uncomfortable racial climate, discrimination, and a lack of contact with African-American faculty (Boyd, 1977).

African-American students in Allen's study characterized their relations with mainstream students as negative. "Unlike their evaluations of specific behaviors for majority faculty or staff, these students did not positively evaluate majority students on any item" (1984, p. 12). African-American students in this study reported that mainstream students avoided interaction with them and questioned their academic ability.

Mentors, Role Models

Administrative and faculty advocates, role models, mentors and persons who act as liaison are needed to decipher an unfamiliar academic culture. Fleming (1984) concluded that mainstream colleges and universities really do not address the adjustment issues faced by African-American students when they move from predominantly African-American to White ones. According to Fleming, mainstream institutions downplay the need for adjustment.

Most students regard mentors as vital to their success (Hall and Allen, cited in Clewell, 1987). Yet, African-American students seldom receive this type of personal guidance from their professors (Blackwell, 1981). Nettles (1990), however, found that Black students perceived mentor support more positively than did majority students. He further observed that students who had the most interaction with faculty were most satisfied with their doctoral programs. Nettles' (1990) findings regarding mentor support were inconsistent with those of Clewell and other researchers. The inconsistency underlines the need for continuing research on these issues.

Adams describes assistantships as the "major outlet for gaining the training needed to enter the professional ranks" (1988, p. 5). Yet, Allen (1982; 1984) found that even when making satisfactory progress, many minority students had not been provided with the opportunities or experiences required to adequately compete in the job market. These experiences included paper presentations at professional meetings, opportunities for co-authorship, papers, acceptance of papers for publication, collaboration on research projects and funding for research.

Social Experiences

Minority graduate students commonly reported social isolation, alienation and lack of adequate support systems as areas of ongoing concern. Nettles' (1990) review of the literature revealed that social experiences were the greatest influence on persistence and performance in graduate school. These experiences are so important that they "mitigate the [positive] effects of undergraduate education and graduate school performance" (p. 4). This is relevant to Allen's research findings which revealed that African-Americans possessed negative perceptions in regard to their interactions with majority students and were ambivalent about mainstream faculty.

Conversely, African-American students reported their interactions with African-American faculty as "excellent" or "good." Unfortunately, an overwhelming majority of these students (the number in parentheses indicates their percentage) thought that there were insufficient numbers of African-American faculty (100 percent); African-American staffs (88 percent), and African-American students (91 percent) at their university (Allen, 1984, p. 14).

Financial Support

Finances are reported as especially important to many minority students who often cannot rely on extensive financial support from home. More specifically, African-American students tend to work full-time, generally attend graduate school part-time and at an older age than their mainstream counterparts. Consequently, family obligations and finances related to ongoing household support are factors that seemingly exacerbate an already precarious financial situation and influence the decision of whether to matriculate and persist (Clewell, 1987). Scott (1981) states that most African-American students come from poor families with little or no financial resources. Therefore, financial support for room, board and books is just as important as that for tuition. Family commitments also pose a major potential hindrance (Allen, 1981).

The students in Nettles' (1990) study who expressed significantly greater feelings of discrimination (in part) tended not to have scholarships or assistantships. "Black students were significantly less likely to receive teaching or research assistantships than either majority or Hispanic students, despite applying for them" (p. 1). Scott (1981) maintains that African-American graduate students often find federal grants inaccessible to them at mainstream schools. Fellowships and assistantships enhance interaction between students and faculty. This type of interaction is also related to doctoral grade point average and perceived satisfaction with doctoral programs. Additionally, even though personal resources such as savings and loans from parents were more often reported as the primary source of support available to African-American and mainstream students, African-American students were more likely to use loans to finance educational costs.

Full-time attendance in graduate school appears to be related to success, yet African-Americans more often attend graduate school part-time and wait longer before enrolling (Nettles, 1990).

Discrepancies between what students perceive as their needs, and what they really need provide additional insight into the reasons that mainstream institutions are unable to demonstrate more success in recruitment and retention at the doctoral level.

Middle Class Status as a Factor

Traditionally, the most frequently used criteria for minority recruitment has inadvertently ensured that little risk is involved for the university. The students who were accepted were almost always those with the greatest chances of succeeding. They tended to be students with "high standardized test scores and [demonstrated] academic achievement" (Thomas cited in VANT, 1988). Along with exemplary performance at the undergraduate level, many of these students report high professional achievement goals, high self-concept and are from homes wherein families have a demonstrated record of academic and professional achievement (Allen, 1984). The families of these students are often middle class, and their parents relatively well-educated. These students have a demonstrated record of leadership as evidenced by their involvement in extra curricular activities (Clewell, 1987). However, even with the available pool of students who are academically talented (as evidenced by past school performance in academic settings), their retention rates in mainstream higher education institutions have been disappointing, and their attrition rates high. The percentage of minorities who fail to complete an undergraduate degree is substantially higher than for mainstream noncompleters

(Clewell citing Astin, 1975 and 1982; Astin and Cross, 1981; Commission on the Higher Education of Minorities, 1982). There is some evidence that similar factors impact undergraduate and graduate level retention (Boyd, 1977).

Based on a review of the literature, VANT and Associates observed that to successfully participate in graduate or professional school study, "students must have high inclinations toward middle class values and accept the system which is structured for the middle class individual" (1988, p. 6). Unfortunately, the majority of "middle class" African-American students are from homes where parents are themselves first generation middle class. This first generation status renders the stability of the position tenuous. Additionally, African-Americans who are middle class often continue to have direct contact with family members who have not yet attained middle-class status. This involvement may weaken the unquestioned adoption of middle-class values and thought required for success in academe.

Many middle-class individuals routinely provide financial assistance to family members in the lower classes to assist in their daily survival. This financial commitment impacts discretionary income and further erodes the stability of middle-class economic status. It is often said that many middle class African-Americans are one paycheck away from poverty.

Despite media images to the contrary, Smythe (cited in VANT, 1988, p. 5) notes that blacks "still ascribe to intelligence, hard work, the right connections, talent, natural leadership, the ability to mix easily with Whites and stick up for one's rights as of major importance to succeeding as a career professional". The overwhelming desire to succeed and to prove themselves capable with mainstream populations seems a definite motivational factor in persistence for African-American students (Allen, 1982; Allen, 1984). The fragile nature of the middle-class economic status, the need to adopt mainstream values to succeed in academe, and the perceived negative environmental factors within institutions, may additionally impact and negatively influence recruitment and retention efforts.

Contributions of Historically Black Institutions

Traditionally, it has been historically Black institutions that have demonstrated success with students deemed to have marginal or deficient skills. The accomplishments of these schools are particularly noteworthy in that mainstream public institutions generally have had greater access to resources such as facilities and capital. These institutions have frequently taken African-American students (including those identified as being educationally disadvantaged) and incorporated strategies to prepare them for success in higher education. However, integration has eroded the enrollments of many of these institutions, and many academically superior students are now choosing to attend mainstream institutions. Historically Black institutions were left to educate many of the students who were considered by mainstream institutions to be academically incapable of succeeding. Yet, the percentage of students who completed degree programs was often higher in these historically Black institutions than in mainstream institutions. Asa Hilliard refers to this as "power teaching: turning silver into gold" (1990). The downside of this situation, however, is that historically Black institutions do not have large numbers of programs at the doctoral level.

Recommended Recruitment and Retention Strategies

The strategies recommended by administrators, researchers, and minority students to lessen the recruitment and retention gap are fairly clear. Institutions need a clearly defined policy on retention, institutional commitment to retention initiatives, improved support services such as counseling and advising, and commitment and support throughout the institution, but especially at the faculty and departmental levels (Collison, 1987). Guiding these initiatives should be a respected individual with widespread support within the university and the department to ensure attention to detail, and to encourage and monitor the progress of currently enrolled students and prospective applicants. This person can also assist deciphering and interpreting barriers to success (Isaac, 1986).

The presence of minority faculty is vital to recruitment and retention efforts. These faculty can provide a degree of support and reference against which minority students can check perceived discrepancies in the academic, personal and social arenas. Women and minorities have serious difficulties finding mentors (Levinson, 1978). Minority faculty would help fill the void. The presence of minority faculty would also allow a perspective that more closely approximates that of minority students (Isaac, 1986; Adams, 1988).

However, recruitment and retention efforts should not be the exclusive responsibility of minority faculty. A concerted effort involving minority and majority professionals is required. It must also be understood that minority faculty face serious issues of their own within academe. Minority faculty are often disproportionately involved in these efforts, but they must be given credit in the university reward structure for their contributions. For example, in a study involving 500 Black faculty in Florida, 84 percent had been offered tenure track positions at the time they were hired, but of this number, 70 percent did not receive tenure. The conclusion reached was that if "there is a direct correlation between tenure and job security, most Black faculty possess little or no job security" (Kolbert, 1989, p. 4). Students would also like to see minorities used more frequently to recruit minorities (Clewell, 1987).

Students responding to Clewell's research (1987) requested that more comprehensive and encompassing indicators be used when evaluating ability for graduate school. Both qualitative and quantitative measures should be used (Adams, 1988).

Students desire an environment that supports dialogue between them and faculty members. They support groups that can encourage the sharing of experiences and promote a sense of belonging. Students desire faculty who are sensitive to the sometimes unique needs of doctoral students.

Processes that facilitate appeals of decisions and actions should be established. In addition, all students should have accessibility to resources and professional information (Allen, 1984).

Ensuring adequate financial aid would also assist in retention (and recruitment) efforts (Isaac, 1986). Upton and Pruitt (1985) suggest that financial aid be separated between minority and non-minority students, with aid specifically being designated for African Americans. Their reasoning stems from racial differences in financial aid distribution. When possible, teaching and research assistantships should be included as a part of the financial aid package to foster closer collaboration between students and professors (Adams, 1988). By this means, students would have a viable and stable source of support. They would also be provided with opportunities to present papers at professional conferences and to gain invaluable experience. Adequate funding would enable students to devote more time to study and research, and alleviate much of the stress associated with financial anxieties.

Summary

Despite the best expressed efforts of universities, "questions linger regarding sincerity of effort and commitment [to] the recruitment and retention of minorities" (Adams, 1988, p. 5). Despite the strategies that have been identified, the bottom line remains the same: results that fall far short of the identified goals.

Several things seem clear, however. Despite the rhetoric surrounding this issue, little has changed within institutions. Separation prevails (Mingle cited in VANT, 1988). African-American students who enroll have a strong desire to succeed and face many obstacles in their quest for the graduate degree. Once enrolled, they are willing to endure tremendous personal sacrifice, isolation, alienation and financial hardship rather than to experience failure. African-American students are often motivated by mainstream individuals to prove that they can succeed (Allen, 1982). Yet, motivation and desire may not be enough to ensure success. "Students in advanced graduate degree programs benefit most when they are able to take full advantage of the professionalization process." Informal relationships that facilitate "ongoing academic discourse, exposure to role models and involvement in profession-related activities" are vital to the process (Allen, 1984, p. 19). When this process does not allow total inclusion, the student is placed at a disadvantage. This disadvantage extends after graduation to the professional networks which often enhance career success.

The decision of the minority student to withdraw from school is one that exacts a great personal toll. The attitude of faculty within a program may be of major impact in the decision of the student to continue.

It can be argued that minority and mainstream graduate students experience similar problems on university campuses. For example, one minority student respondent described faculty as nondiscriminatory. She observed that faculty treated all students alike—like third class citizens (Clewell, 1987). The addition of minority status into this situation, however, may render the experiences of minority graduate students to be unique and particularly difficult (Allen, 1984). For African-American students, the perceived injustices that accompany their graduate school experience may pose the final insurmountable obstacle.

3

Socializing Undergraduates for the Graduate Experience

It has been 20 years since the Adams case was filed by the NAACP Legal Defense Fund (LDF) on behalf of Mr. Kenneth Adams of Mississippi. The suit, which aimed at eliciting a change in former President Richard Nixon's policy of non-enforcement of federal desegregation laws and policies, prohibited federal funds from being distributed to any institution that discriminated on the basis of race, color or national origin (Williams, 1988). The case of Adams v. Richardson (1973) forced the Department of Health, Education and Welfare (DHEW) to respond to the non-action of the Nixon Administration's policy that had, by this time, extended to the primary and secondary levels of education (Williams 1988). This legal action placed the issue of desegregation of American higher education on the public agenda in a serious way for more than a decade.

However, after 1980, it was no longer a critical issue because of the change in national leadership and the continuing conservative shift of the American polity. The Reagan Administrations (1980-1988) did not see the need for continuing the quest of desegregating the traditionally White institutions (TWIs) and further enhancing the historically Black colleges and universities (HBCUs).

Based on the considerable experience of one of the authors, Israel Tribble, Jr. as a consultant to the Office of Civil Rights and as a higher education administrator, it became clear that the Adams litigation and all of its attendant issues really boiled down to something much more fundamental than physical improvements, new degree programs and what race of students would attend what institution.

I strongly argued that the issue of desegregating American higher education centers around the development of a significant pool of Ph.D.s who are African American, Latino American and Native American. This pool of new Ph.D.s must be ready to become "prime time" players in American higher education. Thus, the way that you desegregate American higher education is to produce as many African American and other historically disadvantaged minority Ph.D.s as possible in the shortest possible time. A somewhat small improvement was made in this area as the United States Department of Education reported a significant gain in degrees awarded to minorities in the 1980s. And, small gains were made by students of color at every degree level from 1989 to 1990 (American Council on Education [ACE] 1992). Any other gains, as mentioned earlier, such as new facilities and programs made through the desegregation process are important but fail to bring about fundamental institutional change. Higher education has an "amoebic" quality which allows it to change form and consistency when threatened while the core continues to remain inviolate. Reduce the threat and it generally returns to business as usual.

Graduate education has remained somewhat of a mystery to many Americans who have not been privileged and fortunate enough to have attended graduate school or have had relatives or acquaintances who have experienced graduate education. It can be argued that it continues to remain somewhat of a mystery to many, especially those from historically disadvantaged groups who are still trying to attain the first college degree as trail blazers for their entire family.

Many would agree however, that the attainment of a degree has, over the years, been devalued. According to Ernest L. Boyer, of the Carnegie Foundation for the Advancement of Teaching, the safest thing one can say about a college diploma is that the student probably has been around the campus for about four years. Boyer argues that on many campuses, because of a so-called reformed curriculum, students have become unclear about not only their options, but also their purpose for being there. In earlier times, reforms worked to reinforce the knowledge of the student, not challenge it adversely (Boyer, 1978). It was also a time in which science and technology and modern history were added to the rigid and required curriculum because society's self-image had expanded, not fragmented as it has today (Boyer, 1978).

It has been interesting to listen to and observe all of the conversations and initiatives related to improving undergraduate education. Rarely, if ever, has there been a focus on the formal preparation and exposure of undergraduates to graduate and professional studies as a significant part of the overall strategy for improving undergraduate education. However, some studies have suggested that the process of selecting a career which requires graduate study should begin as early as kindergarten and preschool (Brown 1987). The quality of high school education has also proved to be a significant determinant regarding minority students' successful transition from undergraduate to graduate study. One of the most interesting trends that has emerged from this equation is that more students who take courses in "other programs" other than humanities and social science go on to graduate and professional study (Brown 1987). Unfortunately, we do not have the luxury of going back to the beginning; participation in graduate study is needed now.

However, the fact remains that more minority students are taking the humanities and social science courses. Even though these students earned a higher percentage of bachelor's degrees than did minority students in other programs (Brown 1987), a seemingly irreversible trend persists. In the last two years, the largest gains being made in enrollment for minority undergraduates are at two-year, rather than four-year institutions. This greatly contrasts with the trend from 1988 to 1990 when African American students made their largest gains at four-year institutions (ACE 1992).

It must be clear to the leaders of higher education that the only thing that a BA or a BS degree is going to do for current and future student populations is to guarantee them some disappointment and keep them at a marginal level as opposed to being on the cutting edge with all of the right advanced training and prerequisites for upward mobility within their field of choice. That is not to say that a bachelor's degree is not important, but it is to say that it has become a stepping stone in terms of educational preparation for the world of work as opposed to a terminal experience. Therefore, it becomes critical within the undergraduate experience that students have an introduction and preparation for this next level of educational engagement.

There has been a clearly definable and historical track record for those who have traditionally succeeded in American higher education. In the main, "the dark and the different" have not had the same kind of success as those majority persons who have come from more affluent backgrounds. Data are very clear that, compared to the majority group, there are some disproportionately negative results for certain groups. Consequently, the progress of various groups differs significantly. Without access to institutions, African-American and other minority students cannot achieve full participation (Mingle, 1987). If this is true throughout elementary and secondary and undergraduate education then it stands to reason that even a greater disproportionate representation will be found at the graduate education level. Therefore, to think that American higher education can be desegregated without somehow revisiting some basic assumptions, restructuring practices and reformulating plans and processes with respect to how the system has operated would be an incorrect diagnosis of the problem.

Even though the above is true, it is viewed by many that a college curriculum which suggests that students have nothing in common is just as flawed as one that suggests that all students are alike (Boyer, 1978). Methods to achieve this standard have focused on introducing all students to events, individuals and literature that have contributed to human gains and losses, and having an understanding of a past from which all of us have come from (Boyer, 1978). A corrected reality of America's past should reflect accurate depictions of the experience of African Americans, Native Americans and Latino Americans.

Taking a look at how access to graduate education works presently and how it has worked traditionally will further clarify the position being fostered. First, there must be the recognition that it has been basically an informal system that has been used to the advantage of the majority group and to those who are oftentimes truly exceptional in terms of their performance at the undergraduate level. But, when one looks at the process, it can immediately be understood that such an informal process provides only a small homogeneous number of individuals accessibility to graduate education in this country compared to the eligible numbers who are not well enough informed or experienced enough to know whether they are interested or capable of being successful.

The question becomes, how does the process work? A professor in a given set of classes that he or she teaches will be struck by a student who has the potential to go on and do well at the graduate level. The way it seems the process has worked in the past and the present is that the professor would then call that student into his or her office or to some other location outside of class and would inform the student that he or she in the professor's view, had the potential to go on to graduate study. Usually what followed that recognition and discussion along with recognition of ability was the identification of a contact person at a university who generally was a colleague or maybe even a classmate of the professor. Through the newly established contact, this student would begin to go through the necessary paperwork to become a graduate student under the tutelage of a colleague of the undergraduate professor who recognized his or her potential—usually at an institution that the professor was somewhat familiar with.

Obviously this process leads to a 98 percent or better exclusionary policy for all the other undergraduates who are sitting in classes with this particular professor. Given the way in which American society has developed, it should be clear that the three societal elements of race, gender and class would have a strong bearing on who generally gets selected to graduate school in this informal system. As the numbers of participants have substantiated over time, poor people, women and historically disadvantaged minorities have not been well represented in graduate programs. Since this is true, the question of whether or not the college's financial and academic programs contribute significantly to the success of socially disadvantaged students has become paramount (Mingle 1987). When one begins to focus on doctoral level education and on the critical disciplines of the sciences, mathematics, and business, you find less and less representation of the affected groups mentioned above. Clearly, this kind of informal system works best for the select few and not the capable many.

Then, what is it that is needed to change the nature of this kind of discriminatory system that hides from so many the familiarization with the graduate education experience? The informal system needs to be replaced by a formalized, structured program that would become a part of the undergraduate co-curricular experience at colleges and universities in America. A formal structured approach to the introduction of this element into the undergraduate experience would ensure that this critical element of the undergraduate experience is made available to the vast majority of students as opposed to a select few. The way in which it is suggested that this formal process be implemented is to start with the first time in college orientation in a given institution. The objective of this orientation is not to confuse and overwhelm these young people who are making the formidable transition from high school to college, but to help them make a connection between the grade point average (GPA) that they are about to achieve and its relationship to the admission decision that will be made when they get ready or when they desire to enter graduate school. Therefore, at rather select intervals during the orientation, these new students would be reminded of how important it is for them to do their best in their major field of study because the society is going to require more education once they have obtained their bachelor's degree. The way in which they meet these increased educational demands of society is by extending their education beyond the BA or the BS degree.

Unfortunately, evidence in recent years shows that rather than being encouraged to excel, students, professors and even universities have been lulled into complacency. Author Chester E. Finn, Jr., a professor of education and policy at Vanderbilt University, explains that the primary reason for educational reform failures at both the K-12 and postsecondary levels, is that for the past decade, such efforts have accomplished so little because they have not succeeded at powerfully affecting students' attitudes and behavior. The role of those who teach play a critical role in what happens to the attitudes and behaviors of students.

In citing numerous surveys, Finn proves again and again that children think they are doing well in school when in actuality they are not. For example, American girls and boys give themselves high marks when asked about their abilities, their educational attainment to date, and the performance they expect from themselves in the future. According to Finn (1992), seventy-five percent stated they are among the best students. Conversely, only 37 percent of students in the same age group in Japan rated themselves among the best (Finn, 1992).

Ordinarily, very few Americans, except for the Stanford and Yale types, actually reap the rewards for excelling. Hence, the need to stress excellence on any level of the educational ladder has fallen on complacent ears. Thus, the cycle of undereducation continues on to higher education institutions where still, only a fraction of the institutions continue to actively seek the admissions of the dissipating pool of truly excellent students (Finn, 1992).

It is estimated that 95 percent of students entering U.S. colleges and universities today wouldn't be admitted anywhere else in the world (Finn, 1992). Because of the educational mediocrity that remains so acute among the college-bound portion of the high school population, researchers have found evidence which suggests that the greatest immunity to improvement is found among these more able students because they are most likely to be influenced by college entry standards (Finn, 1992). There is some truth to Mr. Finn's assertions. However, the openness of the American system is consistent with the American ethos. It is also argued that Mr. Finn is using a rather narrow definition of excellence which may require some redefinition.

In an effort to alleviate this situation, an example of a successful program which encourages students to excel beyond postsecondary degree attainment can be found at the University of California at Berkeley. In a study, the Professional Development Program (PDP) at the University found that previously successful minority students who were in the freshmen-sophomore level mathematics courses were being eliminated from Berkeley's two-year sequence that served as a prerequisite to courses in engineering and the sciences (Treisman 1983).

Like other institutions around the country, U.C. Berkeley had established programs that emphasized tutoring, counseling and faculty advisement to ensure the successful matriculation of minority students. It was found that minority students mistook this advice as mere directives and faculty and staff at the school were ill prepared for working with minority students and their concerns (Treisman 1983). This prompted the university to seek other ways in which to improve the performance of these students for eventual admission into upper level courses.

A program called: "The Intervention Strategy: The Mathematics Workshop" was proposed. The study, which was funded by the Fund for Improvement of Postsecondary Education (FIPSE), introduced the following concepts to meet their objectives of improving minority student performance, particularly at the freshmen level (Treisman 1983).

- Building a community of minority freshmen that is academically oriented and a source of peer support;
- Providing minority students with an extensive orientation to the university, and with ongoing academic advisement;
- Monitoring of student's academic progress and their adjustment to the university environment, and advocating students' collective and individual interests;
- Providing minority freshmen with ongoing supplementary instruction; and
- Linking high school-level and undergraduate-level affirmative action efforts.

To date, the program has been very successful, affecting every aspect of freshmen orientation from significant improvements in grades to higher rates of retention for minority students (Treisman 1983). These tactics could be employed in institutions throughout the country because of one reason, which was U.C. Berkeley's ability to integrate the aims of the program and the character of the institution within which it operates (Treisman 1983).

Other ways which have been suggested as a means for improving undergraduate education, particularly for minority students are pre-college enrichment programs; better coordination between high schools and colleges; systemic orientation programs; increased minority faculty involvement and a greater commitment to positive and effective change by the university (W.R. Allen, 1987).

It is interesting to note that the many calls for improvement in undergraduate education rarely, if ever, address themselves to the introduction and familiarization of the graduate education dimension. Nor can one find a consistent focus on the undergraduate research experience as the precursor for graduate study.

This formalized approach continues into the second year. At this point, all undergraduates with 2.5 GPA's or better would be exposed to a graduate fair which would include all of the graduate programs that exist at the initiating institution or institutions within the immediate vicinity. There should be time set aside on a weekend that these students, with the established GPA cut off or better, would be invited to a central location to visit with representatives of various graduate programs. The purpose of this graduate fair is to learn about the requirements, financial aid and the kinds of career paths that one could take with a particular kind of graduate education experience. This would provide the participants with some sense of what is available at their own institution as well as some of the institutions in the area that had graduate education missions. With this occurring in the second year, it gives the student a chance to make a connection between the earlier reference to the importance of the GPA attained during the first year of undergraduate school and now the requirements that these particular programs have for admission. This also provides the graduate education programs with a potential pool of interested undergraduates and encourages them to look at their own students as the most accessible pool of potential graduate students rather than always going outside the institution to find people who are capable and desirous of the graduate education experience. This says, in effect, that you look at home first and then you cast your net much more broadly.

In the third and fourth years of undergraduate study, students should begin to have the whole notion of "research" demystified. In many ways students think that this is something that happens by some magical manifestation as opposed to ordinary people being able to participate and have success in this lofty pursuit. The way in which this gets accomplished is by providing a myriad of opportunities for undergraduate students to work with professors in laboratories, in the preparation of papers for professional meetings or articles for refereed journals or on research teams working on experiments that are going on in scientific laboratories. Students would get to see in a practical, "hands on" kind of way how these academic pursuits get done. The major objective of this undergraduate research experience is that students begin to understand that they too can participate in this lofty, necessary, and important enterprise called research. It is argued that this kind of structured process will not only improve undergraduate education as it is currently known, but it would also begin to democratize the way in which students are prepared for graduate and professional school opportunities. If students are not aware and knowledgeable, it is then not likely that they are going to make very informed decisions. It is argued here that the way in which the academy has gone about introducing students to the notion of graduate study has not been effective, nor has it been broadly disseminated. The 21st century will require that undergraduate students be better exposed to education beyond the baccalaureate, and that they begin to make decisions much earlier about their participation in the next level of higher education beyond the baccalaureate.

4

The McKnight Model

The McKnight Black Doctoral Fellowship Program (MDF), one of the four programs making up the Florida Endowment Fund for Higher Education (FEF), was begun through the efforts of the McKnight Foundation. The McKnight Foundation is a private charitable organization established and endowed in 1953 by William L. and Maude L. McKnight. With a major focus on education, the Foundation initiated talks with Barbara Newell, the former Chancellor of the State University System of Florida in 1982. These talks led to the establishment of the McKnight Programs in Higher Education in 1984, which were then administered by the Florida Association of Colleges and Universities (Florida Endowment Fund, 1989).

Florida was selected by the Foundation because of the time spent in the state by the McKnights at their winter home and their numerous financial and philanthropic investments. The McKnight Foundation Board of Directors made a decision to make a substantial investment in the educational system of Florida in honor of Mr. McKnight (Clague, 1990). Russell V. Ewald, then Executive Vice President of the McKnight Foundation, outlined a three-phase program for the State of Florida at the 1983 annual meeting of the Florida Association of Colleges and Universities (FACU). The Foundation initially committed a total of $15 million with the understanding that $10 million of the total would represent a challenge grant to be matched by the State of Florida on a two-to-one ratio. That is, for every two dollars provided by the Foundation the State would appropriate one dollar. During the initial stage, the Program was to be administered by FACU. This design brought together a unique "private/public partnership" to enhance the development of African Americans and other historically disadvantaged minorities in higher education in the State of Florida (Florida Endowment Fund, 1989).

The Florida Endowment Fund for Higher Education (FEF) was created by the Florida legislature as a result of a year-long series of meetings between the educational and political leadership within the state. From these meetings, the Foundation determined an agenda that it felt would contribute to the improvement of higher education in Florida well into the 21st century. The agenda outlined below consists of three phases (taken verbatim from Florida Endowment Fund, 1989:5):

Phase One: 1984-1985

- The McKnight Junior Faculty Development Fellowship provides up to $300,000 per year for fellowships designed primarily for non-tenured assistant professors. Priority is given to African American and majority female candidates in underrepresented disciplines. This Program awards twenty (20) fellowships designed to encourage excellence in teaching and research.

- The Centers of Excellence were initially funded for a maximum of $500,000 per year ($100,000 per center) for a three-year period. The Centers develop and implement education enrichment programs that expand the minority student post-secondary applicant pool.

- Articulation and Cooperation Projects were designed to establish communication and cooperation between lower and higher education institutions in Florida. Up to $150,000 per year was provided initially. This composite provided for the development of activities involving educators from lower and higher education.

Phase Two: 1985-1986

- The Challenge Grant was created to develop an endowment fund designed to ensure, at a minimum, the life of the two fellowship programs described above. By December 31, 1986, the challenge was met when the Foundation's grant of $10,000,000 was matched by the State's two appropriations of $2,500,000 each. It was in Phase Two on July 1, 1987, that the Florida Endowment Fund became fully operational.

Phase Three: 1986-1989

- The Private/Public Partnership represents the last phase. The broad purpose of the newly established Fund required the review and evaluation of existing programs, the identification of educational needs and the initiation of new programs to alleviate educational problems. A crucial aspect of this phase is the identification of individuals, foundations and corporations willing to provide further financial support.

> This phase has been embraced with vigor by the Board of Directors and is courageously led by the president of the Florida Endowment Fund. Careful consideration is now being given to a broad range of corporations, foundations and individuals who will invest in the perpetuation of the FEF mission "to provide higher education opportunities for African Americans and other socially disadvantaged minorities."

The three phases that extended from 1984 to the present encompassed the four programs for the first three years (1984-87). In 1987, the Florida Endowment Fund (FEF) began administering three programs: 1) the McKnight Black Doctoral Fellowship Program, 2) the McKnight Junior Faculty Development Fellowship Program and 3) the Centers of Excellence. Although all three programs are designed to address the educational concerns primarily facing African Americans as highlighted in the first chapter, this evaluative study is only concerned with the McKnight Black Doctoral Fellowship Program.

McKnight Black Doctoral Fellowship Model (MDF)

One of the crucial elements in this model that is often overlooked is the "private/public partnership." The model is referred to as "private/public" rather than "public/private" because of the conceptual basis. It is private-public because the genesis of the model and the impetus for action were derived from the private sector, not the public sector. Also of significance was the initial capitalization of the FEF, which was $10 million from the McKnight Foundation (private) and $5 million from the State of Florida (public). It is interesting to note that although the private sector initiated the model and provided a larger share of the financial support, the public was the sector that traditionally had the resources. The public sector has had abundant resources in terms of academic programs and faculty within their universities, but their production of African-American Ph.D.'s has been less than desirable. So the problem was not one of the public higher education sector's not having the financial wherewithal or the academic apparatus, but of how to make that sector more responsive and productive.

Looking at educational change, one finds that major change or reform has seldom, if ever, occurred in American education from within. Change has primarily occurred from external pressure that has forced education institutions at all levels from kindergarten through graduate school to change. Therefore, the private-public partnership has served as an agent for change in graduate education in Florida.

The private-public arrangement has allowed the fellowship program to be administered independently of the state and the State University System, yet has allowed the FEF, through its President, to influence educational policy in Florida both directly and indirectly. The "private-public partnership" was strengthened when administrative powers were shifted from a board of directors made up of FACU members to the FEF Board of Directors. This shift broadened the board's membership beyond that of colleges and universities within the state, including public universities, community college and private institutions (Clague, 1990). The current FEF Board has representation from both the public and private sectors and from both educators and the business community.

The MDF Program, given its private-public partnership, has been able to circumvent much of the bureaucratic red tape that tends to stifle many programs and oftentimes causes displacement of the overall goals. Seidman (1988), in looking at federal bureaucracies, saw managers and other federal functionaries as being controlled by internal management systems that had become unyielding and overburdened with red tape. Bureaucracies, by definition, support the status quo and resist change (Weber,1952). A kind of conservatism comes out of the bureaucratic environment. When one moves outside of that environment, a freedom prevails that allows one to move more quickly, be more creative and be more decisive.

The FEF, and hence the MDF Program, does not operate from within a bureaucracy such as the State of Florida or the State University System. Therefore, decisions can be made quickly and time is not lost working through a bureaucratic labyrinth that characterizes most public and private institutions (Clague,1990). Rather than being encumbered bureaucratically, the FEF has "the ability to leverage the institutional commitment—a force that keeps the pressure on" (Tribble,1988). Concomitantly with the private-public partnership, the administrative structure at the FEF has been by design kept relatively small and "deceptively simple" (Clague,1990). Of course, not having to negotiate a large bureaucracy in itself has allowed for a small and deceptively simple administrative structure to function effectively.

The private-public partnership exemplified by the McKnight Program has had far reaching implications for the graduate education of African-American students in the State of Florida and beyond. Program autonomy and its allowance for flexibility has affected students in every aspect of their education, from the manner in which they were recruited through their graduation. Blackwell (1988) offered the following explanations as reasons why there has been a decline in the presence of African Americans in American graduate education. First, there seems to have been a decline in institutional commitment or a low priority attached to the recruitment of African-American students. When pushed, graduate schools often point to the so-called paucity of "qualified" African-American students. Second, is the inadequacy or complete lack of financial assistance. Blackwell (1988: 419) also listed "the paucity of black faculty, an unfavorable institutional climate,...and faculty indifference to the need for diversity..." as reasons for a decline in African American graduate students.

Recruitment

Given the autonomy and the ability to leverage that has been characteristic of the MDF Program, the traditional excuses given in failing to recruit African-American students successfully into doctoral programs have been taken away. The first thing that is unique about the MDF Program is the criteria set up to determine eligibility for a fellowship. MDF fellowships do not require a specific Graduate

Record Examination (GRE) score or grade point average (GPA). The criteria from the beginning were that the person had to: 1) be a United States citizen, 2) be an African American, 3) be a graduate of a regionally accredited institution and 4) take either the GRE or the Graduate Management Aptitude Test (GMAT). The fact that the MDF Program developed simple straightforward criteria for eligibility to the program grew out of the basic assumptions that underlie the heart of the program. These assumptions, again simple and straightforward, are that the level at which students begin their lives does not necessarily determine where they end up, and barring brain damage, any student can learn. Based on these assumptions, Dr. Tribble tells the McKnight Fellows that they "might be second tier, but they are not second rate." The idea of being second tier but not second rate reflects back on the profile of the doctoral student that has been developed over the years. This profile characterizes the doctoral student as white, male, aggressive, a superstar (as measured by GPA and GRE) and one who looks like the professor who selected him to enter the doctoral program. The assumptions that buttress the recruitment plan further reasons that an African-American student that scores anywhere from 1100 to 1500 on the GRE and has a 3.5 or better GPA does not really need this program. This is not to say that some Black students with scores in the aforementioned range are not taken into this graduate program, it just means that the MDF program is designed for doctoral students with less auspicious scores, but certainly with no less auspicious ability and motivation. The assumption underlying the recruitment criteria was developed from qualitative data and the experiences of President Tribble and other African-American professors and administrators nationwide who have come to believe that there is probably a range of 150 to 200 points below the 1,000 threshold set by the State University System of Florida, where African-American graduate students can successfully perform.

Blackwell (1987) points out that most doctoral programs recruit African-American students locally or regionally at best. The MDF Program recruits nationally. The President of the FEF maintains a national profile as a speaker, panelist and educational consultant. Since the MDF Program is the focal point of his speeches, the program has been provided with significant national exposure.

In 1984, when the program was first started, it was assumed that since 25 awards a year at $15,000 each were available, potential students would line up waiting to take advantage of this marvelous opportunity—all one had to do was to advertise and the applications would flood the MDF Program office. During the first year, the program was advertised in the *Chronicle of Higher Education*, the *Black Collegian* and a few other places. The assumption that students were just waiting for this education bonanza and that advertising would suffice proved false. A close analysis of this recruiting outcome revealed that a far more aggressive effort was needed. First, African Americans have traditionally depended upon word-of-mouth to obtain information. Second, the idea of obtaining a doctoral degree, when looked at from a socio-historical context, is still fairly new for most African Americans. The paucity of African-American doctoral holders in and out of higher education serves to exacerbate the situation. In other words, the lack of role models does not encourage African Americans to aspire toward the doctoral degree, particularly when a disproportionately high number of undergraduate students are the first generation in their family to attend college. Obtaining a baccalaureate degree for most African Americans represents the epitome of their aspirations. Accordingly, many of the African-American students from professional families are opting for advanced degrees in engineering and business, including the MBA, or the more traditional professional choices of black middle-class offspring: medicine and law.

Looking at recruiting from the socio-historical context just discussed, a new set of assumptions emerged that led to an extremely successful recruitment effort. A national recruitment effort was launched predicated on a high profile agenda. In the beginning, President Israel Tribble attempted to speak at various colleges and universities, but soon recognized that it would be impossible to reach out nationally in this manner with a small staff. A decision was reached to contact every president of historically Black colleges and universities by mail and ask them to nominate two graduating seniors and two faculty members from their campus, who they felt could profit from this experience. Although the 30 percent response rate eventually reached has been disappointing, the effort has resulted in some serious applicants. Capitalizing on the word-of-mouth process, Dr. Tribble began to refocus his efforts toward state, regional and national conferences for students and university personnel. Examples included professional meetings of affirmative action officers, student support services personnel, minority affairs administrators and specific conferences and meetings of the Council of Higher Education in Virginia, the Commission on Higher Education in South Carolina, the National Association for Educational Opportunity (NAFEO), the American Association for Higher Education and the American Council on Education. The professional groups and subgroups spread the word about the fellowships. Student were introduced to the MDF Program by professionals and, most importantly, were encouraged to pursue the doctoral degree. A part of Dr. Tribble's message to these professional groups was to not only encourage African-American students to apply for the fellowships, but to also encourage them to enroll in a doctoral program. By 1991, more than 300 African-American students from across the country applied for the 25 MDF's available for that year and a total of 101 applicants were accepted into doctoral programs—the largest number since the program began.

Student Support System

From the standpoint of the McKnight Fellows, the small and deceptively simple structure provided accessibility to FEF President Tribble and his staff. Dr. Tribble and his small staff have assumed the tremendous responsibility of responding to the needs and problems faced by 133 fellows during the course of a year (Clague,1990). However, the system works well. Students feel a sense of importance and they feel they have a strong advocate in the FEF President. Accessibility to the FEF President in itself provides a special sense of security that sets the McKnight Fellows apart from most other graduate students matriculating at Florida universities as well as those from throughout the nation.

Not only does the FEF President and his staff keep in close contact with McKnight Fellows on the various campuses, designated faculty and administrators on each campus serve as liaison persons, working with the FEF and faculty on their campuses. When problems arise, the FEF President contacts the campus liaison persons and works out a resolution (Clague, 1990). In many cases problems are resolved on campus, with the campus liaison person taking the lead. Such a system provides the fellowship holder with a three-layered system of support. One, the traditional avenue in which the student attempts to negotiate the campus bureaucracy and/or faculty within his/her department. The second layer, or campus back-up, is the liaison person. The fellowship holder, when faced with a problem that cannot be resolved through traditional means can call upon the liaison person for help. Third, the student can contact the FEF and get assistance in resolving a campus problem. This "concentric model" of student support has worked effectively, according to the fellows and outside evaluators.

Financial Support

Closely paralleling the support structure provided McKnight Fellows is the financial support the FEF has packaged. Financial support is often viewed as the most important ingredient in the ability of African-American graduate students tocomplete the degree (Blackwell,1987). It is reasonable to state that most African-American students would not attend graduate school without some form of support. Those who are the most successful are individuals who have full financial packages that guarantee funding for a specific period of time so long as performance levels remain within the parameter of fellowship requirements. The MDF Program provides this level of support. The annual stipend for each fellow is currently $11,000, plus up to $5,000 in tuition and fees. The level of funding for each fellow is sufficient so that individuals can devote their time to academic endeavors rather than try to meet financial obligations by holding part-time or full-time positions. Most importantly, fellows can count on support for up to five years. The first three years are provided by the FEF and the last two years are to be provided by the participating university.

After the first five years of successful experience with the program, the FEF was able to leverage an institutional commitment of two years for each fellow from Florida universities. This level of support caused a Florida State University faculty member to refer to the fellowship as the " Mercedes of graduate level stipends." Because of the private-public partnership and the fact that funding derives from an endowment, the year-to-year fellowship funds are not for the most part influenced by politics, budget cuts or factors external to the FEF. Only an economic crisis that would affect the endowment could affect the fellowships and that would probably be over the short term.

Role Modeling/Mentoring/Bonding/Networking

Russell Ewald, formerly of the McKnight Foundation, introduced the idea of an Annual Fellows Meeting for both the McKnight Fellows and the Junior Faculty Fellows. Once the idea of the Annual Fellows Meeting was introduced, President Tribble fully endorsed the concept. Drawing from his graduate experience at Stanford University, President Tribble recognized that a major mission of a program such as the MDF was to uplift, educate, motivate, clarify, and expose the fellows to the graduate school culture as well as its myths. The Annual Fellows Meeting provided an excellent opportunity for such a socialization and motivational process to be initiated. The idea here was that if students could overcome their fears and insecurities and were strong enough to withstand the often unfriendly atmosphere faced by African Americans and other minorities, the academic aspect would take care of itself. In other words, if the McKnight Fellows could learn to cope with or overcome environments in which professors and other graduate students might question their presence as graduate students and reveal doubts about their ability to perform, they could move on to be successful in their chosen fields of study.

In order to tackle these concerns, the decision was made to invite first rate African-American scholars to the Annual Fellows Meeting as role models. These role models would not only demonstrate that success was attainable, but they would also serve as mentors to the fellows. Since 1984, the role models/mentors have discussed many topics related to graduate school and the college teaching profession. Although many of the discussions take place in small informal groups or one-on-one, the following sections presented at Annual Fellows Meetings provide some insight into what has been discussed:

Panels:
- Graduate School Culture
- Women's Issues in Higher Education
- The Role of Black Faculty and Staff Organizations on Campus
- Higher Education: Past, Present and Future
- Career Planning
- Cultural Diversity and the Academy
- Love Jones: The Body Clock and the Graduate Student
- Proposal Writing
- The Future of Historically Black Institutions
- American Higher Education and Diversity: A Meeting of Great Minds

Speakers:
- Professional Responsibilities
- A Continuing Legacy of Excellence
- Blacks in Graduate Education: A Status Report
- Free Your Mind
- The Academic Life: A Sociologist's View
- Towards Pluralism and Excellence: The Task of Black Academicians
- Powerful Teaching and the Professoriate
- Transition from Graduate Student to Faculty Member
- They Came Before Columbus
- African-American Studies in the Nineties: A View from the Trenches
- Hybridity, the Rap Race and Pedagogy for the 1990s

While titles provide some clue to the focus of discussions, the full magnitude of the speeches and panel discussions cannot be portrayed here. Speakers such as Asa Hilliard and Ivan Van Sertima have provided a strong Afrocentric grounding for the fellows.

The Annual Fellows Meeting is always held in a high quality hotel and meals are superb. This is a conscious decision and an integral part of the McKnight Model, because it communicates to fellows that they are special. The Model is designed to instill in the fellows that they are important and deserve the best, but more importantly, that they can do what they have to do to persist through graduation. It is also important that they internalize, as a value, the concept of giving back to others.

Another crucial element in the McKnight Model is the evolution of the Council of Elders. The Council of Elders is made up of senior level African-American faculty and administrators who are available to the fellows at the meetings and also can be consulted by telephone throughout the year. Through the use of the Council of Elders, the FEF has expanded its mentorship capabilities by utilizing individuals from across the country who have distinguished themselves in higher education. Through the annual conference, a support group of peers and role models has emerged (Campbell and Patton,1988).

Probably one of the most important outcomes of the annual conference is the networking and bonding that takes place between the fellows. As a result, when a Fellow is the only African-American student in his/her program, that student does not feel a sense of total isolation. He or she knows that there are other fellows at other institutions that can be called upon for assistance or just to communicate with generally. The MDF Program breaks down the traditional isolation students have felt in the past through its networking. Campbell and Patton(1988:108), during interviews with fellows at the 1987 conference, obtained the following relating to feeling of isolation:

> Because of contacts with the other McKnight fellows, I know that my troubles in adjusting are shared. I am not by myself in pursuing my graduate studies, with so many interested in my success, and so many helping.

> It helps tremendously to know that I am not a Black out there all by myself.

Another Fellow revealed the practical nature of the networking that takes place between fellows (Campbell and Patton,1988:108):

> Each fellow I talk to has provided very practical information in a number of areas that gives me tips on what I can and should expect to encounter and do in my studies, and even afterwards. They tell me things nobody else has told me about what it's like to work on a degree and work for tenure and beyond. If I didn't have the other fellows to tell me how things work, I don't know if I would make it.

From a nonacademic perspective, fellows bond socially, taking part in weddings, providing child care, holding small gatherings routinely in their homes and providing support in times of crisis. One of the fellows, in a letter to President Tribble, discussed how many of the fellows came to his academic rescue and provided psychological support when his father died.

Bonding and networking tend to begin when the fellows first meet. With subsequent meetings the networking expands and the bonding intensifies. It is important to keep in mind that although networking is seen as occurring between graduate students, the networking will continue as fellows become faculty members and as they rise within their professions. One could go so far as to stipulate that the McKnight Fellows have the potential of becoming one of the most powerful professional networks in the country. They will certainly become one of the most powerful African-American doctorates, not tied together by degree, but through the McKnight experience. Interestingly, it will be a network that will constantly expand with each new group of Fellows. Moreover, the fellows as faculty members will send their students to Florida and to the FEF to get the McKnight experience. In this way, not only do you have an ever expanding network, but universities in Florida will have a constant flow of extremely capable

African-American doctoral students.

The annual conference emphasizes the importance of research to the graduate student and to the career of a faculty member. At each conference research topics are discussed and a full session is devoted to research presentation by fellows. The emphasis on research is part of socializing fellows into graduate school culture. Fellows are made to understand that the Ph.D. degree is a research degree and that their success in graduate school and in an academic career will depend to a large degree on their understanding of the research process. The networking that takes place at the conference helps to facilitate research among fellows. They have an opportunity to present their research and to identify other fellows with a similar research interest.

Program Feedback

Program feedback is a formal part of the annual conference, and has proven so important that it will be discussed separately. Much of the change that has taken place in the MDF Program since inception has come from student feedback. The fact that the FEF had the flexibility to change and to respond to newly identified needs of students points once again to the advantage of the private-public partnership. When student feedback from the annual conference identified legitimate needs that could be addressed without compromising the financial or organizational integrity of the program, these needs were quickly met. Had there been an elaborate bureaucratic structure to contend with, change would have been much slower, if at all.

Resulting from student feedback, the socialization process that is designed to expose students to the graduate school culture currently begins during an orientation for new students, is continued during the annual conference and is again provided at a mid-year fellows conference. Originally, the McKnight Fellows were only exposed to the annual conference. During one of the feedback sessions it was brought out that a mid-year conference was needed to reinforce what was covered at the annual conference. From those concerns, the mid-year conference was started in 1988. The mid-year conference is restricted to the McKnight Doctoral Fellows. Outside speakers are not present and the fellows conduct the sessions as well as give the luncheon address. Panels are set up to report on faculty mentor-student mentee relationships and on the research being conducted in the various disciplines represented. Of course the mid-year conference provides another opportunity for networking and bonding between fellows. The Council of Elders are invited as observers, mentors and evaluators.

At the first mid-year conference in 1988 the fellows for that year voiced concern that the 25 new McKnight Fellows should receive an orientation to the McKnight experience and to graduate education prior to entering their graduate programs. The old fellows did not feel the new fellows could afford to wait until the annual conference for an orientation session because a student's first exposure to graduate education could affect the success of that student throughout the program. At the orientation, one member of the Council of Elders is present and gives the new fellows an inspirational talk about the seriousness of graduate education and what they can expect socially and academically. Some of the old fellows are brought in to tell the new fellows about their graduate school experiences both positive and negative. Just as important as the orientation to graduate school, the new fellows have a chance to meet each other and the member of the Council of Elders who is present. Therefore, since 1988, when the orientation was first started, bonding, networking, mentoring and role modeling begins for Mc Knight Fellows prior to their entrance into their graduate program and it continues throughout their graduate school experience. The orientation also gives them a chance to appreciate the depth and breadth of their class and the tremendous potential that they possess individually and collectively.

As a result of the feedback that has been received over the years, McKnight Fellows now have personal computers (PCs), major medical insurance, book allowances and the opportunity to apply for matching travel funds. All these features of the program add to the sense of security, support and well-being experienced by the fellows.

Conclusion

The McKnight Doctoral Fellowship Program, although administered by a lean and deceptively simple administrative structure, has developed into a complex model that is buttressed by sound, but oftentimes what is considered by some mainstream observers as non-traditional, assumptions about graduate education. It is not that these assumptions are new or have just been discovered, they have merely been overlooked as graduate education evolved around the idea that what was good for the majority male students was good for everyone. The McKnight Model is based upon the graduate school experiences faced by African-American doctorates who are currently successful in higher education. Through the feedback system, current McKnight Fellows have had the opportunity to further refine the model as it continues to evolve. Not to be ignored is the fact that the private-public partnership that characterizes the McKnight Program has provided the flexibility necessary for the model to continue developing and maturing.

What the McKnight Program represents is a unique and somewhat novel model in graduate education. Yet traditional values are emphasized, as in the importance of research, the necessity for hard work and the rewards of persistence. Higher education today is abuzz with concepts such as cultural diversity and the need for role models. However, graduate universities have held fast to more traditional criteria for admittance and traditional methods of pedagogy. Universities have attempted to institute new programs designed to increase diversity and new initiatives to attract African-American faculty and administrators as role models. But these efforts have been made without any significant attempts to change the institutional culture (see Richardson, 1989). This is why the McKnight model has emerged as one of the most powerful forces in the production of African-American doctorates. Through its private-public partnership it has been able to leverage important concessions, cooperation and support within graduate education circles in Florida. The institutional culture at Florida graduate universities is changing because of their successful experiences. However, to buttress change, the McKnight model provides a strong support system and its own mechanism for socializing its fellows into the graduate school culture. These features are strong, and they are bringing about the desired result—the increased production of African-American doctorates.

5

The Findings: McKnight vs. Non-McKnight Students

Based upon the McKnight model just presented, it is expected that differences will exist between McKnight and non-McKnight doctoral students matriculating at Florida universities. These differences are expected to exist in terms of recruitment, professional development, financial assistance and support mechanisms.

Data Collection

Considering the fact that the main objective of this study was to evaluate the effectiveness of the McKnight Black Doctoral Program in producing African-American doctoral degree recipients, a decision was made to compare African-American doctoral students attending Florida universities who have received McKnight fellowships with those who have other types of financial support or no support at all. A complete listing of all McKnight fellowship holders was provided by the Florida Endowment Fund for Higher Education, which administers the McKnight Black Doctoral Fellowship Program. By contacting each graduate level institution in the State of Florida that has at least one doctoral program, a complete list of all matriculating African-American doctoral students for the Fall Semester, 1990 was developed. From the list of all African-American doctoral students, the McKnight students were deleted and a complete list of non-McKnight students was established.

Data were collected in two ways. First, questionnaires were mailed directly to all currently matriculating McKnight Fellows. A direct mailing was possible because the files of all McKnight Fellows are updated annually, including a current address. Each McKnight Fellow received a questionnaire and a letter that asked her or him to participate and explained the purpose of the study. Fellows also received a stamped self-addressed envelope in order for them to return the questionnaire. The non-McKnight doctoral students received the same material, however, the method of contacting them differed from that of the McKnight Fellows. Non-McKnight students were contacted by a "point person" from the graduate school of their respective university. Questionnaire packages were mailed with the student's name to the point person at his/her university. The point person contacted each non-McKnight student matriculating at that university and provided them with the questionnaire, the letter and the return envelope.

Of the 135 McKnight Fellows matriculating in Florida universities in the Fall, 1990, 103 or 76.3 percent of the questionnaires were returned. For the non-McKnight students, 133 or 48.2 percent of the 276 students identified and contacted returned usable questionnaires.

Organization of the Findings

The findings are organized around major topical headings that closely relate to the main issues brought out in the literature review as well as the discussion of the McKnight Model. The first section presents a demographic description of the two groups, followed by their educational characteristics. The second section is devoted to a discussion of recruitment. The next section discusses financial support, followed by sections devoted to an analysis of professional development, support systems and institutional quality.

Demographic Characteristics

Gender

Looking at Table 3 below, it was revealed that a statistically significant difference existed between McKnight and non-McKnight students based on their gender. While this difference might not seem important on the surface, given the trends in graduate school participation rates and graduation rates for African-American males, which show a significant decline in both rates between 1976 and 1988, the McKnight gender breakdown seems to be going against this trend. The questionnaire responses revealed that for McKnight Fellows a slightly higher percent of males (51.5) than females (48.5) were enrolled in Florida universities. The non-McKnight gender breakdown more closely corresponded to national trends, with higher percentages of female (61.7) than male (38.3) students. During the review process, there was never an attempt by the FEF to correct for the so-called "male deficit". Clearly, the McKnight Black Doctoral Fellowship Program is addressing the national need for increasing the pool of African-American male doctorates. The long range affect of the increase in male doctorates could have a positive effect on the production of future recipients in that they will serve as role models for young African-American males and in turn encourage them to stay in school and aspire toward graduate degrees.

Urban-Rural Background

The fact that for both McKnight and non-McKnight students larger percentages were from urban backgrounds is not surprising. Since 1940, migration trends have drastically altered the urban-rural dichotomy for African Americans. The rural based Black population in America during the early part of the 20th century has become an urban-based Black population today (see Jaynes and Williams, 1989). According to Table 3, 71.3 percent of the McKnight students and 66.9 percent of the non-McKnight students were born in urban areas.

Table 3:
Demographic Characteristics of McKnight Fellows and Non-McKnight Students

Educational Characteristics	**McKnight Fellows**		**Non-McKnight Students**	
Demographic Variables	**Number**	**%**	**Number**	**%**
Gender [1]				
Female	50	48.5	82	61.7
Male	53	51.5	51	38.3
TOTAL	**103**	**100**	**133**	**100**
Urban-Rural Background [2]				
Urban	72	71.3	87	66.9
Rural	29	28.7	43	33.1
TOTAL	**101**	**100**	**130**	**100**
Marital Status [3]				
Married	35	34	74	55.6
Single	53	51.5	40	30.1
Divorced / Separated	15	14.5	17	12.8
Widowed	0	0	2	1.5
TOTAL	**103**	**100**	**133**	**100**

Table 3 (cont):
Demographic Characteristics of McKnight Fellows and Non-McKnight Students

Educational Characteristics	McKnight Fellows		Non-McKnight Students	
Demographic Variables	**Number**	**%**	**Number**	**%**
Age[4]				
Under 25	12	11.7	7	5.3
25-29	33	32.0	20	15.0
30-34	23	22.3	22	16.6
35-39	18	17.5	43	32.3
40 and Over	17	16.5	41	30.8
TOTAL	**103**	**100**	**133**	**100**
Social Class Status[5]				
Upper Class	1	1.0	3	2.3
Middle Class	36	34.9	41	30.8
Working Class	53	51.5	73	54.9
Lower Class	12	11.6	16	12.0
No Answer	1	1.0	0	0
TOTAL	**103**	**100**	**133**	**100**

[1]X^2 = 4.048: with 1df (Significant at the.05 level)
[2]X^2 = .505: with 1df (Not significant at the .05 level)
[3]X^2 = 14.314 with 3df (Significant at the .003 level)
[4]X^2 = 21.233: with 4df (Significant at the .001 level)
[5]X^2 = 2.294 with 4df (Not significant at the .05 level)

Marital Status

Again referring to Table 3, a significant difference was found between the marital status of McKnight and non-McKnight students, the major difference being that 51.5 percent of the McKnight students were single and 55.6 percent of the non-McKnight students were married. The higher percentage of single McKnight students could translate into fewer nonacademic obligations and responsibilities and hence, more time to devote to succeeding in graduate school. Conversely, the higher percentage of non-McKnight students who were married, could mean that these students have been encumbered with family obligations and responsibilities that have created a heavy burden in addition to their academic requirements.

Age

According to Table 3, 42.7 percent of the McKnight students were under 30 years of age whereas only 20.3 percent of the non-McKnight students fell into this age bracket. These data are in keeping with the previous finding that higher percentages of McKnight students are single than married, while the opposite was found to be true for non-McKnight students. At this point, McKnight students can be characterized as more likely to be young, male or female, single and from urban backgrounds, while the non-McKnight students can be characterized as more likely to be older, female, married and from urban backgrounds.

Social Class Status

Social class status differences between the two groups were not found (see Table 3). Approximately the same percentages for each class strata were found for both groups. The largest percentage of McKnight Fellows (51.5) and non-McKnight students (54.9) were in the working class. Also, of some importance was the fact that approximately 12 percent of both groups identified themselves as coming from lower-class backgrounds, with almost none of the Fellows or students indicating upper-class family backgrounds.

The importance of this finding is that the McKnight Doctoral Fellowship Program has not been recruiting students from middle and professional family backgrounds in proportions that are higher than normal recruiting trends within the State of Florida. Studies have shown that students from upper-status families are more likely to attain more education (Epps and Jackson, 1988), take college preparatory classes in mathematics and science (Lee, 1985) and be encouraged and supported by parents and teachers (Sewell et al, 1970). In other words, children from upper- and middle-class families, because of more exposure and parental support and encouragement, tend to reach higher levels of education than children from working- and lower-class families. Assuming the findings from previous studies are valid and if the McKnight Black Doctoral Fellowship Program recruited from the middle and upper classes, then one could say that its success was due to the type of students brought into the Program. However, one of the major tenets of the McKnight Model is "that the level at which an individual began his/her life does not necessarily determine where they end up and barring brain damage any student can learn." These data clearly show that McKnight Fellows do not come from elite backgrounds and supports the above stated tenet.

Table 4:
Educational Background of Parents/Guardians of McKnight Fellows and non-McKnight Students

Educational Characteristics	McKnight Fellows		Non McKnight Students	
Educational Background of Guardian with the Highest Grade Completed	**Number**	**%**	**Number**	**%**
Elementary School	4	.39	16	11.9
Some High School	16	15.5	24	17.9
High School Graduate	16	15.5	34	25.4
Some College	22	21.4	24	17.9
College Graduate	15	14.6	15	11.2
Post College	30	29.1	21	15.7
TOTAL	103	96.49	134	100

Educational Background of Parent

The respondents were asked to provide the educational level of their parent or guardian who had attained the most education. Looking at Table 4, a significant difference was found between the McKnight Fellows and the non-McKnight students. Contrary to what would have been expected, given the social class status of the McKnight Fellows and the non-McKnight students, the educational background of the parent with the most education for the McKnight Fellows was significantly higher than non-McKnight Fellows. Approximately 29 percent of the McKnight Fellows had a parent or guardian with some post-college education, while only 15.7 percent of the non-McKnight students had a parent similarly educated. Of the non-McKnight students, 29.8 percent of the parents with the highest educational level had not finished high school. For the McKnight Fellows, the percentage not finishing high school was 19.4. Overall, for both McKnight Fellows (56.3 percent) and non-McKnight students (43.1 percent) a greater number of the parents with the most education had not finished college when compared to those parents that had finished.

Although these data provide a somewhat different picture than was found pertaining to social-class status, one can clearly see that the McKnight recruits were from a cross-section of the African-American student population, and not just from elite backgrounds. Actually, McKnight recruits were more likely to be from lower- and working-class status backgrounds. There are two explanations that can be offered to illustrate the differences between social-class status and parental education. First, studies have shown that African Americans tend to downgrade their subjective (self-selected) class status (Goyder and Pineo, 1974; Heiss and Owens, 1972). Second, and somewhat related, is the fact that African Americans receive a smaller financial return on their educational attainment than their White counterparts (see Jaynes and Williams, 1989). Therefore, the educational level attained as a single indicator of class status can be misleading.

Educational Characteristics of Respondents

Undergraduate Institution Attended

Table 5 reveals whether or not the respondents from both groups attended a historically Black college or university (HBCU) or a historically majority college or university (HMCU).

Table 5:
Educational Characteristics of McKnight Fellows and Non-McKnight Students

Educational Characteristics	McKnight Fellows		Non-McKnight Students	
College--Bachelor's Degree[1]	Number	%	Number	%
Historically Black	65	63.7	75	57.7
Historically White	36	35.3	54	41.5
Foreign	1	1.0	1	.8
TOTAL	102	100	130	100
Undergraduate Grade Point Average[2]	Number	%	Number	%
4.00 - 3.75	11	10.8	5	3.8
3.74 - 3.50	17	16.7	23	17.6
3.49 - 3.25	15	14.7	17	13.0
3.24 - 3.00	20	19.6	30	22.9
2.99 - 2.75	26	25.5	30	22.9
2.74 - 2.50	8	7.8	19	14.5
2.49 - 2.25	4	3.9	4	3.0
2.24 - 2.00	0	-	3	2.3
No Answer	1	1.0	-	-
TOTAL	102	100	131	100

Table 5 (cont):
Educational Characteristics of McKnight Fellows and Non-McKnight Students.

Educational Characteristics	McKnight Fellows		Non-McKnight Students	
Previous Graduate Degree[3]	**Number**	**%**	**Number**	**%**
Yes	66	64.1	108	81.2
No	36	34.9	25	18.8
No Answer	1	1.0	-	-
TOTAL	103	100	133	100
Master's Grade Point Average[4]	**Number**	**%**	**Number**	**%**
4.00 - 3.75	17	26.2	28	26.2
3.74 - 3.50	23	35.4	45	42.0
3.49 - 3.25	14	21.5	19	17.8
3.24 - 3.00	9	13.9	15	14.0
2.99 - 2.75	2	3.0	0	-
TOTAL	65	100	107	100

[1] $X^2 = .949$; with 2df (Not significant at the .05 level)
[2] $X^2 = 10.597$; with 8df (Not significant at the .05 level)
[3] $X^2 = 9.461$; with 2df (Significant at the .01 level)
[4] $X^2 = 4.050$; with 4df (Not significant at the .05 level)

A significant difference was not found between the McKnight Fellows and non-McKnight students based on whether they attended a HBCU or a HMCU. It is interesting to note that a higher percent of the McKnight Fellows (63.7) and the non-McKnight students (57.7) received their baccalaureate degrees from HBCUs. More than forty HBCUs were among those attended by McKnight Fellows and non-McKnight students. These institutions represented a wide range of HBCUs, including such schools as: Grambling, Talledega, Benedict, Paine, Tuskegee, Florida A&M, North Carolina Central, Knoxville, Morehouse, Savannah State, Spelman, Hampton, Edward Waters, Delaware State, and Tennessee State.

Undergraduate Grade Point Average

As can be seen from Table 5, a significant difference was not revealed between the grade point averages (GPA) obtained by McKnight Fellows and non-McKnight students while attending undergraduate school. Approximately 62 percent of the McKnight Fellows and 57.3 percent of the non-McKnight students completed their undergraduate studies with GPAs of 3.00 and above. Of those with GPAs of 3.00 and above, the highest percentage was in the 3.00 to 3.24 category. This was true for both groups. Approximately 25 percent of the McKnight Fellows with GPAs below 3.00 were in the 2.99 to 2.75 category and 22.9 percent of the non-McKnight students were similarly categorized.

It is important to note that McKnight and non-McKnight students performed similarly as undergraduates. If the McKnight Fellows had revealed significantly higher GPAs than non-McKnight students, then it might have been concluded that the success of the McKnight Fellows was due to selective recruitment rather than the supportive design of the program, as outlined in the model presented earlier. Also of importance, is the fact that 37.2 percent of the McKnight Fellows and 42.7 percent of the non-McKnight students completed their undergraduate education with GPAs that were less than 3.00 These data tend to support the McKnight Model and others (Blackwell, 1988; Claque, 1990; Pruitt and Issac, 1985) who have maintained that graduate school performance is not tied solely to grades or GRE scores.

Previous Graduate Degree

Looking at Table 5, a significant difference was found between the McKnight Fellows and the non-McKnight students that had completed a graduate degree prior to entering their doctoral program. For McKnight Fellows, the percent having already obtained a graduate degree was 64.1. This finding was closely related to the earlier discussion about GPAs. Students who have already completed graduate degrees, provide some indication that they can succeed at that level. Again, evidence was provided that indicated that the success of the McKnight Black Doctoral Fellowship Program was not due to the recruitment of students who were more likely to succeed than that of more traditional programs, as reflected by the non-McKnight students. To the contrary, traditional programs were more likely to have recruited students into the doctoral program that had already completed a graduate degree than was the case for the McKnight Program.

Master's Grade Point Average

Of the McKnight and non-McKnight students who had completed graduate degrees prior to entering a doctoral program, there was not a significant difference in their GPAs. The top GPA category (4.00-3.75) had the same percent (26.2) of McKnight and non-McKnight students. A slightly higher percentage of non-McKnight students (42.2) than McKnight Fellows (35.4) had GPAs in the 3.74 to 3.50 category and almost identical percentages of both groups had attained GPAs in the 3.24 to 3.00 category.

Based on the educational characteristics of students from both groups, as revealed in Table 5, the success of the McKnight Black Doctoral Fellowship Program cannot be attributed solely to the kind of students recruited. These data clearly show that significant differences were not present between McKnight Fellows and non-McKnight students, except in terms of those having already received a graduate degree. In that case, significantly higher percentages of non-McKnight students than McKnight Fellows had already acquired graduate degrees. Preliminarily, these data seem to be indicating that factors related to the McKnight model account for the success of the McKnight Black Doctoral Fellowship Program.

Undergraduate Major

Table 6 provides a look at the undergraduate majors of the McKnight Fellows and non-McKnight students. A significant difference was found between the two groups. For McKnight Fellows, undergraduate majors in which the highest percentages were reflected were in biology (14.6), computer science/engineering (10.7), psychology (10.7), physics (7.8) and mathematics (6.8). Non-McKnight students, on the other hand, were more likely to have majored as undergraduates in education (14.3), psychology (12.8), business (9.8), communication/mass communication (7.5) and sociology (6.0). These data indicate that McKnight Fellows were, as undergraduate majors, clustered in the pure and applied sciences more so than the non-McKnight students. Looking at non-McKnight students, one sees undergraduate majors along more traditional lines for African Americans, in education and social sciences.

Table 6:
Undergraduate Major of McKnight Fellows and Non-McKnight Students

Educational Characteristics	McKnight Fellows		Non-McKnight Students	
Undergraduate Major	**Number**	**%**	**Number**	**%**
Education	5	4.9	19	14..3
Economics	2	1.9	2	1.5
Geography	1	1.0	1	.8
Crinimal Justice	1	1.0	4	3.0
History	3	2.9	3	2.3
Interdisciplinary Social Science	1	1.0	1	.8
Political Science	2	1.9	7	5.3
Psychology	11	10.7	17	12.8
Sociology	1	1.0	8	6.0
Social Work	-	-	4	3.0
Public Administration	-	-	1	.8
Anthropology	1	1.0	-	-
African-American Studies	-	-	1	.8
Communication Mass Communications	5	4.9	10	7.5
English/Languages	6	5.8	7	5.3
Art	-	-	3	2.3
Theater	2	1.9	-	-

Table 6 (cont):

Undergraduate Major of McKnight Fellows and Non-McKnight Students

Educational Characteristics	McKnight Fellows		Non-McKnight Students	
Undergraduate Major	**Number**	**%**	**Number**	**%**
Music	1	1.0	4	3.0
Religion	-	-	1	.8
Theology	-	-	1	.8
Library Sciences	-	-	2	1.5
Human Development/Family Studies	1	.9	2	1.5
Health Sciences	1	.9	2	1.5
Nursing	5	4.9	3	2.3
Pharmachology	1	1.0	1	.8
Physical Therapy	1	1.0	1	.8
Physics	8	7.8	2	1.5
Mathematics	7	6.8	2	1.5
Biology	15	14.6	3	2.3
Chemistry	5	4.9	6	4.5
Computer Science / Engineering	11	10.7	1	.8
Construction Technology	-	-	1	.8
Agriculture	1	1.0	-	-
Business	5	4.9	13	9.8
TOTAL	103	100.3	133	100.7

X^2 = 66.018; with 34df (Significant at the .001 level)

Given that the McKnight Black Doctoral Fellowship Program (MDF) placed a high emphasis on areas of national need and areas in which African Americans have not traditionally majored, these data were not surprising. What was surprising, was that the MDF Program had been successful in its quest to identify students with backgrounds in the sciences, behavioral sciences and other non-traditional areas. The success of the MDF Program revealed that African-American students in non-traditional areas were available. However, non-traditional efforts have to be employed to identify and recruit these students.

Campus Organizations

Vant and Associates (1988) pointed out that social isolation was a factor that affects whether or not Black students attend graduate school. Wilson and Justiz (1989) saw isolation as a factor affecting persistence. McKnight Fellows and non-McKnight students were asked to provide the number of campus organizations they were active in as undergraduate students (see Table 7). A significant difference was not found between the two groups. A slightly higher percent of

Table 7:
Number and Percent of Campus Organizations McKnight Fellows and Non-McKnight Students Were Active as Undergraduates

Educational Characteristics	McKnight Fellows		Non-McKnight Students	
Number of Campus Organizations Active in As Undergraduate	**Number**	**%**	**Number**	**%**
None	20	19.2	23	17.3
One	8	7.8	27	20.3
Two	36	35.0	42	31.6
Three	19	18.5	19	14.3
Four	8	7.8	8	6.0
Five or More	12	11.7	14	10.5
TOTAL	103	100	133	100

$X^2 = 7.446$; with 5df (Not significant at the .05 level)

McKnight Fellows (11.7) stated they were active in five or more undergraduate campus organizations than non-McKnight students (10.5). However, a slightly higher percentage of McKnight Fellows (19.2) indicated no active involvement when compared with non-McKnight students (17.3). When examining the number of students being active in three or more campus organizations as undergraduates, 38 percent of McKnight Fellows and 30.8 percent of the non-McKnight students indicated that level of activity.

These data revealed that both McKnight Fellows and non-McKnight students were active in campus organizations as undergraduate students. Their activity provides a possible clue to the degree of isolation experienced by both groups. It seems that McKnight Fellows (80.8 percent) were involved in campus organizations; and non-McKnight students revealed a slightly higher percentage (82.7) of involvement. Having been active in campus organizations could have been a factor in both their decision to enter graduate school and their persistence once there. Campus involvement reflected a possible lack of isolation while on campus. The implications of these findings for graduate study would be different for both groups based on whether or not their undergraduate studies took place at a historically Black or historically majority institution. Those who attended a HMCU and were active as undergraduates would probably be better able to adjust in graduate programs at a HMCU.

Recruitment

Applications to Doctoral Programs

Table 8 shows the number of doctoral programs the McKnight Fellows and the non-McKnight students applied to prior to their admittance. A significant difference was found between the two groups, with a higher percentage of McKnight Fellows (66.0) applying to more than one program than non-McKnight students (41.0).

Approximately 20 percent of the McKnight Fellows had applied to four or more doctoral programs, while only 12.7 percent of the non-McKnight students had made that many applications.

One possible factor that could account for the differences found between these two groups, was the fact that many non-McKnight students did not have the level of financial support that the McKnight Fellows had; therefore, they were geographically bound and only applied to the local institution with a doctoral program. The McKnight Black Doctoral Fellowship Program, on the other hand, encourages its applicants to apply to as many as three Florida institutions that offer the doctoral degree in their area of interest. More light will be shed on this explanation when financial support is discussed.

Table 8:
Number and Percent of Doctoral Programs Applied to by McKnight Fellows and Non-McKnight Students

Educational Characteristics	McKnight Fellows		Non-McKnight Students	
Number of Doctoral Programs Applied To	**Number**	**%**	**Number**	**%**
One	35	34.0	79	59.0
Two	26	25.2	23	17.2
Three	22	21.4	15	11.2
Four	7	6.8	4	3.0
Five	1	1.0	3	2.2
Six	5	4.9	2	1.5
Seven or More	7	6.8	8	6.0
TOTAL	103	100	134	100

X^2 = 17.913; with 6df (Significant at the .01 level)Table 8

Acceptance into Doctoral Programs

Continuing to analyze the process of entering doctoral programs, Table 9 revealed the number of programs to which McKnight Fellows and non-McKnight students received acceptance. As would be expected, given the differences in the number of programs applied to between the two groups, 59.2 percent of the McKnight Fellows were accepted into two or more programs. For the non-McKnight students, only 31.1 percent were accepted into two or more programs. This difference was also significant. Approximately 5 percent of the McKnight Fellows were accepted into seven or more programs and none of the non-McKnight students received that many favorable responses.

Table 9:
Number and Percent of Doctoral Programs that Accepted McKnight Fellows and Non-McKnight Students

Educational Characteristics	McKnight Fellows		Non-McKnight Students	
Number of Doctoral Programs Accepted into	**Number**	**%**	**Number**	**%**
One	42	40.8	91	68.9
Two	33	32.0	25	18.9
Three	15	14.6	11	8.3
Four	5	4.9	3	2.3
Five	3	2.9	1	.8
Six	-	-	1	.8
Seven or More	5	4.9	-	-
TOTAL	103	100	132	100

X^2 = 24.059; with df (Significant at the .001 level)

Doctoral Degree Institutions

Two major factors influenced attendance at doctoral granting universities in Florida. One factor was the number of doctoral programs offered by an institution, and the second factor was the fields of study available. The University of Florida, Florida State University and University of Miami offered the most doctoral programs, and hence, a wide variety of fields. Florida A&M University and Barry University each only offer one doctoral program.

Table 10 shows which universities McKnight Fellows and non-McKnight students were enrolled in as doctoral students. A significant difference was found between the two groups. For McKnight Fellows, 34.3 percent were at the University of Florida and 30.4 percent were at Florida State University. The higher percentage of McKnight Fellows at Florida A&M emphasizes the push of the MDF Program toward the pure and applied sciences or related fields. Conversely, Nova University, which is included under other universities, has a large graduate program in education and thus accounted for many of the 17.2 percent of the non-McKnight students in that category. Since most universities in Florida that offer doctoral programs have one in education, non-McKnight students attended a greater variety of institutions than McKnight Fellows.

Table 10:

Florida Universities Where McKnight Fellows and Non-McKnight Students Are Currently Pursuing Doctoral Degrees

Educational Characteristics	McKnight Fellows		Non-McKnight Students	
University Currently Enrolled in and Pursuing Doctoral Degree	**Number**	**%**	**Number**	**%**
Florida A&M University	10	9.8	1	.8
Florida Atlantic University	1	1.0	5	3.7
Florida International University	2	2.0	5	3.7
Florida State University	31	30.4	44	32.8
University of Central Florida	1	1.0	3	2.2
University of Florida	35	34.3	6	4.5
University of Miami	11	10.8	26	19.4
University of South Florida	9	8.8	17	12.7
Barry University	1	1.0	4	3.0
Other Universities	1	1.0	23	17.2
TOTAL	102	100	134	100

$X^2 = 62.399$; with 9df (Significant at the .001 level)

Most Influential Person

Table 11 indicates the person who was most influential in the decision of McKnight Fellows and non-McKnight students to attend graduate school to pursue a doctoral degree.

A significant difference was not found between the two groups. According to McKnight Fellows, 28.2 percent of them were most influenced by a college professor, 27.2 percent by a parent guardian and 23.3 percent were not influenced by anyone. Similar individuals were mentioned by non-McKnight students, however, the order varied. For non-McKnight students, "no person was influential" was the most common response (27.6 percent), followed by parent/guardian (23.9 percent) and other (20.9 percent).

Table 11:
Person Most Influential in the Decision of McKnight Fellows and Non-McKnight Students to Pursue the Doctoral Degree

Educational Characteristics	McKnight Fellows		Non-McKnight Students	
Person Most Influential	**Number**	**%**	**Number**	**%**
Parent(s) or Guardian	28	27.2	32	23.9
Sibling	3	2.9	3	2.2
Other Relative	3	2.9	6	4.5
College Professor	29	28.2	25	18.7
Minister	1	1.0	1	.8
Teacher (other than College Professor)	-	-	2	1.5
Other	15	14.6	28	20.9
No person was influential	24	23.2	37	27.6
TOTAL	103	100	134	100

$X^2 = 6.317$; with 7df (Not significant at the .05 level)

Factor Most Influential

Looking at factors that were most influential in the decision made by McKnight Fellows and non-McKnight students to pursue the doctoral degree, a significant difference was not found (Table 12). For McKnight Fellows (52.4 percent) and non-McKnight students (69.4 percent) personal ambition/motivation was overwhelmingly the most frequently mentioned factor. This finding clearly indicated that African-American graduate students pursued doctoral degrees for personal reasons rather than more altruistic reasons such as being a role model.

Table 12:
Factors Most Influential in the Decision of McKnight Fellows and Non-McKnight Students to Pursue the Doctoral Degree

Educational Characteristics	McKnight Fellows		Non-McKnight Students	
Most Influential Factor	**Number**	**%**	**Number**	**%**
Personal Ambition/Motivation	54	52.4	93	69.4
Status Recognition	4	3.9	2	1.5
Economic Value of Education	4	3.9	6	4.5
Role Model for Other African-American Youths	13	12.6	12	9.0
Teach in Higher Education	14	13.6	13	9.7
Become a Researcher	7	6.8	4	3.0
Other	7	6.8	4	3.0
TOTAL	103	100	134	100

$X^2 = 9.230$; with 6df (Not significant)

Financial Support

Importance of Financial Support

A significant difference was found between McKnight Fellows and non-McKnight students in terms of whether or not they would have been able to attend graduate school without financial assistance. Referring to Table 13, an overwhelming number of McKnight Fellows (71.8 percent) and non-McKnight students (61.7 percent) indicated they would not have been able to pursue graduate studies without financial assistance. However, it is interesting to note that 18.8 percent of the non-McKnight students and only 2.9 percent of the McKnight Fellows stated they would have been able to attend graduate school without assistance. Although more data will be presented within the report that will help explain this difference, one would be inclined to speculate that many non-McKnight students were currently attending graduate school without financial support. Therefore, they would have answered "yes" that they could attend without assistance.

Table 13:
Number and Percent of McKnight Fellows and Non-McKnight Students Who Would Have Been Able to Attend Graduate School

Educational Characteristics	McKnight Fellows		Non-McKnight Students	
Attend Graduate School Without Financial Assistance	**Number**	**%**	**Number**	**%**
Yes	3	2.9	24	18.8
Not Sure	26	25.3	25	19.5
Definitely Not	74	71.8	79	61.7
TOTAL	103	100	128	100

$X^2 = 13.974$; with 2df (Significant at the .001 level)

Graduate Education Financed

Prior to discussing Table 14, it is necessary to reiterate how the McKnight Black Doctoral Fellowship Program works. McKnight Fellows receive full funding from the Florida Education Fund for the first three years of their doctoral study. If a Fellow needs additional time to finish the degree, and almost all doctoral students nationally need more than three years, the participating institution picks up the last two years at the same level of funding provided by the FEF. An important aspect of the McKnight Model, brought out earlier, was the ability of the FEF President to negotiate with Florida doctoral granting institutions. The additional two years of support by the institutions resulted from negotiations between the FEF President and appropriate individuals at each of the participating universities.

Looking at Table 14, these data clearly show the level of financial support provided by the FEF to the McKnight Fellows. Approximately 54 percent of the McKnight Fellows stated that 90 percent of their current graduate education was financed through their fellowship. Slightly over 19 percent of the McKnight Fellows stated that between 90 and 75 percent of their funding came from their fellowship. The 6.8 percent of the McKnight Fellows who stated they did

Table 14:
How Current Graduate Education Is Financed by Number and Percent

	Over 90%		90% - 75%		75% - 50%		50% - 25%		25% - 10%		10% - 0%		Did Not Rec.		2	df	Sign
Source of Support	N0.	%	No.	%	No.	%	No.	%	No.	%	No.	%	No.	%	Values		Levels
McKnight Fellowship	55	53.4	20	19.4	12	11.7	9	8.7	-	-	-	-	7	6.8			
University Fellowship																	
McKnight Fellow	-	-	-	-	-	-	-	-	4	3.9	-	-	99	96.1	23.768	10	.01
Non-McKnight Student	5	3.7	11	8.2	-	-	8	6.0	5	3.7	3	2.2	102	76.1			
University Teaching Assistant																	
McKnight Fellow	-	-	2	1.9	-	-	3	2.9	-	-	4	3.9	94	91.3	11.563	12	n.s.
Non-McKnight Student	5	3.7	2	1.5	2	1.5	4	3.0	1	3.0	1	.8	116	86.6			
University Research Assistant																	
McKnight Fellow	1	1.0	-	-	-	-	5	4.6	4	3.9	2	2.0	91	88.4	4.569	12	n.s.
Non-McKnight Student	2	1.5	1	.8	2	1.5	3	2.2	4	3.0	1	.8	121	90.3			
State Fellowship																	
McKnight Fellow	-	-	-	-	-	-	1	1.0	-	-	1	1.0	101	98.1	6.206	10	n.s.
Non-McKnight Student	1	.8			2	1.5	2	1.5	3	2.2			126	94.0			
U.S. Government Fellowship																	
McKnight Fellow	-	-	-	-	-	-	1	1.0	1	1.0	-	-	101	98.1	6.206	10	n.s.
Non-McKnight Student	4	3.0	1	.8	1	.8	-	-	2	1.5	-	-	126	94.0			
Private Fellowship (Non-McKnight																	
McKnight Fellow	-	-	-	-	-	-	-	-	-	-	2	1.9	101	98.1	10.365	12	n.s.
Non-McKnight Student	1	.8	1	.8	3	2.2	2	1.5	5	3.7	1	.8	121	90.3			
Personal Savings																	
McKnight Fellow	-	-	-	-	-	-	2	1.9	2	1.9	9	8.7	90	87.4	24.410	12	.02
Non-McKnight Student	11	8.2	5	3.7	7	5.2	5	3.7	5	3.7	16	11.9	85	63.4			

McKnight Fellows (N=103) and non-McKnight Students (N=134)

Table 14 (cont):
How Current Graduate Education Is Financed by Number and Percent

Source of Support	Over 90%		90% - 75%		75% - 50%		50% - 25%		25% - 10%		10% - 0%		Did Not Rec.		2	df	Sign
	N0.	%	No.	%	No.	%	No.	%	No.	%	No.	%	No.	%	Values		Levels
Veteran's Education Benefits																	
McKnight Fellow	-	-	-	-	-	-	-	-	-	-	-	-	103	100	3.158	-	-
Non-McKnight Student	-	-	-	-	-	-	2	1.5	2	1.5	-	-	130	97.0			
Loans																	
McKnight Fellow	-	-	-	-	-	-	1	1.0	3	2.9	11	10.7	88	85.4	28.191	12	.01
Non-McKnight Student	12	9.0	4	3.0	8	6.0	6	4.5	8	6.0	6	4.5	90	67.2			
Part-time University Work																	
McKnight Fellow	1	1.0	-	-	2	1.9	-	-	1	10.	5	4.9	94	91.3	44.338	10	.001
Non-McKnight Student	-	-	-	-	1	.8	5	3.7	2	1.5	8	6.0	118	88.1			
Part-time Outside Work																	
McKnight Fellow	-	-	-	-	1	1.0	4	3.9	5	4.9	7	6.8	86	83.5	2.375	12	n.s.
Non-McKnight Student	1	.8	1	.8	1	.8	5	3.7	6	4.5	6	4.5	114	85.1			
Parents																	
McKnight Fellow	-	-	-	-	1	1.0	1	1.0	3	2.9	9	8.7	89	86.4	64.662	8	.001
Non-McKnight Student	-	-	-	-	-	-	-	-	-	-	10	7.4	124	92.5			
Spouce's Earnings/Mone																	
McKnight Fellow	-	-	-	-	1	1.0	4	3.9	3	2.9	5	4.9	90	87.4	6.529	10	n.s.
Non-McKnight Student	3	2.2	-	-	5	3.7	2	1.5	2	1.5	9	6.7	113	84.3			
Other																	
McKnight Fellow	-	-	-	-	1	1.0	-	-	-	-	4	3.9	98	95.2	15.296	12	n.s.
Non-McKnight Student	6	4.5	2	1.5	3	2.2	8	6.0	1	.8	6	4.5	108	80.6			

not receive any funding from the MDF Fellowship were students in their fourth and fifth years. Although they did not receive funding directly from the FEF, McKnight Fellows (N=103) and non-McKnight students (N=134) received funds equivalent to the McKnight Fellowship from the institution they were attending. As was mentioned earlier, these funds were arranged by the FEF.

For the non-McKnight students, 23.9 percent received some level of funding through a university fellowship, with the highest percent (8.2) stating that this accounted for between 90 and 75 percent of their current funding. Less than 10 percent of the non-McKnight students stated they received any level of funding from either of the following sources: university research assistantships, state fellowships, U.S. Government fellowships, private fellowships (non-McKnight), veteran's benefits, or parents. The two sources from which non-McKnight students were more likely to receive support included personal savings (36.6 percent) and loans (32.8 percent). Personal savings (8.2 percent) and loans (9.0 percent) were also sources in which non-McKnight students stated they received over 90 percent of their current funding. The fact that this many non-McKnight students stated that they depended on savings and loans for over 90 percent of their funding, supports the early speculation that many of the non-McKnight students who stated they would have been able to attend graduate school without financial assistance, were already supporting themselves.

These data clearly show one important difference between McKnight Fellows and non-McKnight students, and that is their level of financial assistance. One important ingredient in the McKnight model was financial security. McKnight Fellows were funded for up to five years at a level that would allow most students to pursue their doctoral studies without the distraction of working or being overly concerned about financial matters. Given that McKnight Fellows were also provided with a contribution toward their health insurance, their tenure in graduate school was relatively secure financially.

Non-McKnight students exemplified the financial crisis most African-American and other minority students face while pursuing graduate degrees. Research assistantships and teaching assistantships, a primary source of funding for doctoral students, are often difficult for African-American students to obtain. These data indicated that only 13.4 percent of the non-McKnight students had university teaching assistantships and 9.7 percent had university research assistantships. By far, too many of the non-McKnight students had to depend upon personal sources of funding.

Availability of Institutional Funding

In Table 15 respondents were asked whether or not they were satisfied with the level of financial assistance provided at their university. There was a significant difference found between McKnight Fellows and non-McKnight students. A higher percent (47) of McKnight Fellows stated they were either satisfied or very satisfied and 36.5 percent of the non-McKnight students expressed similar sentiments. Conversely, 37.2 percent of the non-McKnight students expressed some level of dissatisfaction, and 25 percent of the McKnight Fellows had similar expressions.

Table 15:
Availability of Financial Assistance from Current University Based on the Perception of McKnight Fellows and Non-McKnight Students

Educational Characteristics	**McKnight Fellows**		**Non-McKnight Students**	
The extent to which financial assistance has been available through your program, department or university	**Number**	**%**	**Number**	**%**
Very dissatisfied	6	6.0	24	18.6
Dissatisfied	19	19.0	24	18.6
Somewhat satisfied	18	18.0	34	26.4
Satisfied	38	38.0	30	23.3
Very satisfied	19	19.0	17	13.2
TOTAL	100	100	129	100

$X^2 = 13.907$; with 4 df (Significant at the .01 level)

One has to keep in mind that the McKnight Fellows did not have to depend upon their university for financial support until the fourth year into their doctoral program and then the level of funding was the same as that provided by the FEF. Therefore, it is reasonable to assume that many of the McKnight Fellows viewed university financial assistance from how they were funded, when in actuality there were wide variations in the funding levels provided non-McKnight students. Referring back to Table 14, approximately 25 percent of the non-McKnight students did not receive any funding from their university. These students had to depend on personal savings, loans, spouse's earnings and their employment for over 90 to 100 percent of their financial support while pursuing doctoral studies.

Professional Development

Opportunities for Professional Growth and Development

Table 16 revealed attitudes expressed by McKnight Fellows and non-McKnight students to a series of questions that were designed to determine how well their current university provided for their growth and development. The first question asked about the overall academic progress McKnight Fellows and non-McKnight students were making in their program. A significant difference between the two groups was not found. Only 5.8 percent of McKnight Fellows and 6.2 percent of non-McKnight students voiced any level of dissatisfaction.

The next question asked to what extent McKnight Fellows and non-McKnight students felt their program was helping them meet their professional goals. Table 16 does not reveal a significant difference between the two groups concerning this question. An overwhelming percent of both groups expressed some level of satisfaction in attaining their professional goals through their program.

Continuing to look at Table 16, McKnight Fellows and Non-McKnight students were asked if opportunities for professional growth and development were provided at their university. Again a significant difference was not found between the two groups. A slightly higher percent of non-McKnight students (14.6) were either dissatisfied or very dissatisfied than McKnight Fellows (12.6 percent).

Finally, both groups were asked if courses were available to them that met their professional needs and interests. Referring back to Table 16, a significant difference was not found. Although the differences were slight, non-McKnight students were more likely to express dissatisfaction (15.9 percent) than McKnight Fellows (9.7 percent). These data clearly showed that both McKnight Fellows and non-McKnight students felt their current university was helping them grow and develop professionally.

Table 16:
Attitudes Toward Professional Growth and Development of McKnight Fellows and Non-McKnight Students

Educational Characteristics	McKnight Fellows		Non-McKnight Students	
Attitudes Toward Professional Growth and Development	**Number**	**%**	**Number**	**%**
The overall academic progress you feel you are making in your program				
Very Dissatisfied	4	3.9	3	2.3
Dissatisfied	2	1.9	5	3.9
Somewhat Disatisfied	23	22.3	34	26.2
Satisfied	50	48.5	53	40.7
Very Satisfied	24	23.3	35	26.9
TOTAL	**103**	**100**	**130**	**100**
The extent to which your program of studies is preparing you to attain your professional goals				
Very Dissatisfied	2	1.9	3	2.3
Dissatisfied	8	7.8	7	5.4
Somewhat Disatisfied	18	17.5	26	20.0
Satisfied	56	54.4	58	44.6
Very Satisfied	19	18.5	36	27.7
TOTAL	**103**	**100**	**130**	**100**

Table 16 (cont):
Attitudes Toward Professional Growth and Development of McKnight Fellows and Non-McKnight Students

Educational Characteristics	McKnight Fellows		Non-McKnight Students	
Attitudes Toward Professional Growth and Development	**Number**	**%**	**Number**	**%**
Opportunities provided by your program for professional growth and development				
Very Dissatisfied	2	1.9	3	2.3
Dissatisfied	11	10.7	16	12.3
Somewhat Disatisfied	28	27.2	39	30.0
Satisfied	41	39.8	47	36.2
Very Satisfied	21	20.4	25	19.2
TOTAL	**103**	**100**	**130**	**100**
The opportunity to take courses that meet your professional needs and interests				
Very Dissatisfied	4	3.9	4	3.0
Dissatisfied	6	5.8	17	12.9
Somewhat Disatisfied	35	34.0	27	20.5
Satisfied	39	37.9	60	45.5
Very Satisfied	19	18.5	24	18.2
TOTAL	**103**	**100**	**132**	**100**

Professional Organizations/Societies

McKnight Fellows and non-McKnight students were asked if they had joined a professional organization or society since starting their doctoral program. Table 17 clearly revealed that a significant difference did not exist between the two groups. Approximately 49 percent from each group had joined a professional organization or society.

Table 17:
McKnight Fellows and Non-McKnight Students Who Joined Professional Organizations/Societies Since Starting Doctoral Programs

Educational Characteristics	McKnight Fellows		Non-McKnight Students	
Professional Organizations/Societies	Number	%	Number	%
Yes	50	49.0	65	48.5
No	52	51.0	69	51.5
TOTAL	**102**	**100**	**134**	**100**

$X^2 = .006$; with 1df (Not significant)

Professional Meetings/Conferences

Table 17 showed that about one half of both groups had joined a professional organization or society since entering their doctoral program. Of course, having joined an organization or society is indicative of professionalism. Attending professional meetings and/or conferences also reflects professionalism.

Looking at Table 18, an interesting trend begins to emerge. Approximately 87 percent of the McKnight Fellows stated they had attended a professional meeting/conference since starting their program, while only 39.9 percent of the non-McKnight students indicated likewise. This difference was significant. Although not shown graphically, the two groups were also asked to list up to three professional meetings and/or conferences. The McKnight Annual Conference was defined as a professional meeting, and all the McKnight Fellows except those that were in their first year listed the conference. Of equal importance was that 87 different professional meetings and conferences were listed, and McKnight Fellows had attended most of those listed. Non-McKnight students listed two or three conferences or meetings they had attended, however, the frequency of attendance was far less than that of McKnight Fellows. Of course, the higher frequency of attendance at conferences for the McKnight Fellows was

Table 18:
McKnight Fellows and Non-McKnight Students Who Attended Professional Meetings/Conferences Since Starting the Doctoral Program.

Educational Characteristics	McKnight Fellows		Non-McKnight Students	
Professional Meetings/Conferences	**Number**	**%**	**Number**	**%**
Attending Since Starting Doctoral Program				
Yes	89	87.3	53	39.9
No	13	12.7	80	60.1
TOTAL	**102**	**100**	**133**	**100**
Meeting Beneficial to Academic Work				
Yes	84	95.5	47	89.0
No	4	4.5	6	11.0
TOTAL	**88**	**100**	**53**	**100**
Able to Network with Other Students				
Yes	81	92.0	31	57.4
No	7	8.0	23	42.6
TOTAL	**88**	**100**	**54**	**100**
Provided Employment Information				
Yes	73	82.9	27	50.9
No	15	17.1	26	49.1
TOTAL	**88**	**100**	**53**	**100**
Left More Determined to Finish the Doctoral Program				
Yes	80	94.1	45	86.5
No	5	5.9	7	13.5
TOTAL	**85**	**100**	**52**	**100**

due to the travel fund provided by the FEF.

Returning to Table 18, of those from both groups who had attended a professional meeting and/or conference, the overwhelming sentiment was that it was beneficial to their academic work. A significant difference between the two groups was not found.

Of extreme importance to the successful completion of graduate work, is the ability to network with other students. An important ingredient in the McKnight Model is the ability of McKnight Fellows to network with each other. Furthermore, the model states that networking begins with the McKnight Orientation and the Annual Conference and continues throughout the graduate educational experience. These data support this assumption that is so crucial to the model. Ninety-two percent of the McKnight Fellows stated that they were able to network with other students, and only 57.4 percent of the non-McKnight students were able to network. It is reasonable to assume that this significant difference between the two groups was due in part to the McKnight Conferences.

Providing further support to the contention that McKnight Conferences were a factor accounting for differences in networking, were the differences shown in Table 18 in whether or not the conference or meeting provided employment information. Almost 83 percent of the McKnight Fellows stated they were provided employment information at their conferences or meetings and only 50.9 percent of the non-McKnight students stated the same. An important feature of the McKnight Annual Conference are the displays and representatives from various colleges and universities from around the country. Not only is information available, recruiters from different colleges and universities seek out McKnight Fellows. Many institutions have representatives in attendance in an attempt to identify promising McKnight Fellows during the early part of their doctoral program and closely follow them through to completion. The idea is that by staying in close contact, the institution is in a much better position to hire the individual when his/her work is completed.

A significant difference was not found between McKnight Fellows and non-McKnight students in whether or not they left the conference or meeting more determined to finish their doctoral program. A little over 94 percent of the McKnight Fellows and 86.5 percent of the non-McKnight students stated they were more determined to finish their degree after having left a conference or meeting.

Current Grade Point Averages

Table 19 shows that a significant difference was not found between the two groups, based upon their grade point averages (GPA). However, it is interesting to note that a slightly higher percentage of McKnight Fellows (25.5) than non-McKnight students (22.1) had GPAs in the 4.00 to 3.75 range. Within the 3.74 to 3.50 range, 39.8 percent of the non-McKnight students and 30.9 percent of the McKnight Fellows indicated having GPAs in this range.

Table 19:
Current GPAs of McKnight Fellows and Non-McKnight Students

Educational Characteristics	McKnight Fellows		Non-McKnight Students	
Grade Point Averages--Doctoral Program	Number	%	Number	%
4.00-3.75	24	25.5	25	22.1
3.74-3.50	29	30.9	45	39.8
3.49-3.25	25	26.6	23	20.4
3.24-3.00	12	12.8	16	14.2
2.99-2.75	3	3.2	-	-
2.74-2.50	1	1.1	1	.9
2.49-2.25	-	-	2	1.8
2.24-2.00	-	-	1	.9
TOTAL	94	100	113	100

$X^2 = 8.462$; with 7df (Not significant at the .05 level)

It is not surprising that significant differences in GPA were not found between the two groups. In graduate school students have to maintain a 3.00 GPA to remain in their program and to finish. Approximately 96 percent of the McKnight Fellows and 96.4 percent of the non-McKnight students had GPAs that were 3.00 or better.

However, it is important to keep in mind that the McKnight Fellows were attaining GPAs equal to non-McKnight students despite being enrolled in non-traditional doctoral programs for African Americans. As an example, approximately 50 percent of the McKnight Fellows were enrolled in the sciences, mathematics, engineering and computer science whereas over 50 percent of the non-McKnight students were enrolled in education. Of course, the McKnight Black Doctoral Fellowship Program does not accept applications for graduate study in education except in math and science education.

Year Entered Doctoral Program

Although a significant difference was not found between McKnight Fellows and non-McKnight students and the year they entered their doctoral program (see Table 20), noteworthy differences can be pointed out. Since the MDF Program accepts 25 new students each year and they are supported by the FEF and their university for up to five years, one can glean some idea of the differences in years toward graduation between the two groups.

Table 20 reveals that of the McKnight Fellows who responded to this survey, 88.3 percent were within the five years of continued FEF and university support. Conversely, 7.8 percent of the McKnight Fellows were in their sixth year of study, and only 4.5 percent of the non-McKnight students were in their sixth year. However, for the seventh and eighth (or more) years, only 2.9 percent and 1.0 percent respectively of the McKnight Fellows were still pursuing their degree. Of the non-McKnight students, on the other hand, 5.2 percent were in their seventh year and 5.2 percent were in their eighth year or more. According to statistical data maintained by the FEF, the average time to degree completion for McKnight Fellows is four years and six months.

Table 20:
Year McKnight Fellows and Non-McKnight Students Entered Doctoral Programs

Educational Characteristics	McKnight Fellows		Non-McKnight Students	
Academic year entered Doctoral Program	Number	%	Number	%
Prior to 1984	1	1.0	7	5.2
1984-1985	3	2.9	7	5.2
1985-1986	8	7.8	6	4.5
1986-1987	14	13.7	11	8.2
1987-1988	12	11.8	23	17.2
1988-1989	18	17.7	35	26.1
1989-1990	22	21.6	21	15.7
1990-1991	24	23.5	24	17.9
TOTAL	102	100	134	100

$X^2 = 11.552$; with 7df (Not significant at the .05 level)

Isolation on Campus

Opportunity to Study and Solve Problems

Looking at Table 21 reveals whether or not McKnight Fellows and non-McKnight students had opportunities to study or problem solve with other graduate students at their university. Approximately 92 percent of the McKnight Fellows and 83.6 percent of the non-McKnight students indicated that they had opportunities to study or problem solve with other students. This difference, however, was not significant.

Of those students from the two groups who stated that they had opportunities to study or problem solve with other students from their university, a question was asked about the race/ethnicity of those with whom they studied or problem solved. Approximately 74 percent of the McKnight Fellows and 63.4 percent of the non-McKnight students stated they only studied with mixed race/ethnic groups. Only

7.4 percent of the McKnight Fellows stated they studied with other African-American graduate students, but 20.5 percent of the non-McKnight students identified African-American graduate students. This difference was also not significant.

Table 21:
Opportunities of McKnight Fellows and Non-McKnight Students to Study/Solve Problems

Educational Characteristics	McKnight Fellows		Non-McKnight Students	
Opportunity to study/solve problems	**Number**	**%**	**Number**	**%**
With graduate students at your university*				
Yes	93	91.2	112	83.6
No	9	8.8	22	16.4
TOTAL	**102**	**100**	**134**	**100**
If yes, were they:*				
African-American	7	7.5	23	20.5
Other Minority	2	2.2	3	2.7
White	15	16.1	15	13.4
Mix (different race/ethnic group)	69	74.2	71	63.4
TOTAL	**93**	**100**	**112**	**100**

* Not significant at the .05 level

Table 21

Assigned Group Projects

Both groups were asked if they were ever assigned to group projects by a professor at their university. For non-McKnight students, 66.9 percent stated they were and 54.4 percent of McKnight Fellows indicated likewise (see Table 22). This difference was not significant. Also not significant, was whether or not the two groups were ever assigned to mixed racial/ethnic groups. Of the students who had been assigned to study groups, 89 percent of the McKnight Fellows and 91.1 percent of non-McKnight students stated that they had been assigned to mixed groups.

Table 22:
McKnight Fellows and Non-McKnight Students Who Were Assigned Group Projects by the Professor

Educational Characteristics	McKnight Fellows		Non-McKnight Students	
Assigned group projects by professor	Number	%	Number	%
At your university*				
Yes	55	54.5	89	66.9
No	46	45.5	44	33.1
TOTAL	**101**	**100**	**133**	**100**
If yes, group(s) mixed racically/ethnically*				
Yes	49	89.0	82	91.1
No	6	11.0	8	8.9
TOTAL	**55**	**100**	**90**	**100**

* Not significant at the .05 level

Table 22

Shared Information

Table 23 reveals whether or not McKnight Fellows and non-McKnight students shared course-related information with other students at their university and with students from other Florida universities. A significant difference was not found.

Ninety-six percent of the McKnight Fellows and 91 percent of the non-McKnight students shared course-related information with students from their university. A slightly higher percentage of McKnight Fellows (35.3) than non-McKnight students (25.4) had shared information with students from other Florida universities. The slightly higher percent of McKnight Fellows that shared information with students from other Florida universities could have been due to the networking that takes place between the Fellows.

Table 23:
McKnight Fellows and Non-McKnight Students Who Shared Information

Educational Characteristics	McKnight Fellows		Non-McKnight Students	
Shared information related to course	**Number**	**%**	**Number**	**%**
With students at your university*				
Yes	96	96.0	122	91.0
No	4	4.0	12	9.0
TOTAL	**100**	**100**	**134**	**100**
With students from other Florida Universities*				
Yes	36	35.3	34	25.4
No	66	64.7	100	74.6
TOTAL	**102**	**100**	**134**	**100**

* Not significant at the .05 level

Table 23

Support Systems, Role Models and Mentoring

Attitudes Toward Support Systems, Networking and Bonding

Table 24 provides data from a series of questions aimed at determining attitudes of McKnight Fellows and non-McKnight students toward support, networking and bonding. Data are shown that reflect concern displayed by faculty in the academic progress and interests of the two groups. No significant difference was found, however, almost twice the percentage (19.6) of the non-McKnight students over McKnight Fellows (10.7) voiced some level of dissatisfaction.

Next, the two groups were asked about "The peer support network you have been able to establish." A significant difference was found. Approximately 31 percent of the McKnight Fellows stated they were very satisfied with the peer support network they had established, and only 17.6 percent of the non-McKnight students answered in the same

Table 24:
Attitudes of McKnight Fellows and Non-McKnight Students Toward Support Systems, Networking and Bonding.

Attitudes Toward Current University	McKnight Fellows		Non-McKnight Students	
Support/Networking/Bonding	**Number**	**%**	**Number**	**%**
The concern shown by faculty in your academic progress and interests				
Very Dissatisfied	3	2.9	9	6.8
Dissatisfied	8	7.8	17	12.8
Somewhat Disatisfied	30	29.1	29	28.1
Satisfied	42	40.8	54	40.6
Very Satisfied	20	19.4	24	18.1
TOTAL*	**103**	**100**	**133**	**106**
The peer support network you have been able to establish				
Very Dissatisfied	1	1.0	7	5.3
Dissatisfied	10	9.7	24	18.3
Somewhat Disatisfied	30	29.1	36	27.5
Satisfied	30	29.1	41	31.3
Very Satisfied	32	31.1	23	17.6
TOTAL**	**103**	**100**	**131**	**100**
The opportunities to meet other students who share the same interests as you				
Very Dissatisfied	0	0	2	1.5
Dissatisfied	11	10.7	22	16.9
Somewhat Disatisfied	36	34.9	30	23.1
Satisfied	42	40.8	52	40.0
Very Satisfied	14	13.6	24	18.5
TOTAL*	**103**	**100**	**130**	**100**

Table 24A

Table 24 (cont):
Attitudes of McKnight Fellows and Non-McKnight Students Toward Support Systems, Networking and Bonding.

Attitudes Toward Current University	**McKnight Fellows**		**Non-McKnight Students**	
Support/Networking/Bonding	**Number**	**%**	**Number**	**%**
Opportunities to bond with other students				
Very Dissatisfied	1	1.0	9	6.8
Dissatisfied	10	9.7	25	18.9
Somewhat Disatisfied	40	38.8	38	28.8
Satisfied	39	37.9	45	34.1
Very Satisfied	13	12.6	15	11.4
TOTAL**	**103**	**100**	**132**	**100**
The availability of someone to assist you in resolving a problem faced on campus				
Very Dissatisfied	1	1.0	8	6.2
Dissatisfied	15	14.6	21	16.2
Somewhat Disatisfied	27	26.2	33	25.4
Satisfied	42	40.8	47	36.1
Very Satisfied	18	17.5	21	16.2
TOTAL*	**103**	**100**	**130**	**100**
The psychological support you have received since entering your current program				
Very Dissatisfied	1	1.0	14	10.8
Dissatisfied	17	16.7	26	20.0
Somewhat Disatisfied	31	30.4	28	21.5
Satisfied	32	31.4	40	30.8
Very Satisfied	21	20.6	22	16.9
TOTAL**	**102**	**100**	**130**	**100**

Table 24B

Table 24 (cont):
Attitudes of McKnight Fellows and Non-McKnight Students Toward Support Systems, Networking and Bonding.

Attitudes Toward Current University	McKnight Fellows		Non-McKnight Students	
Support/Networking/Bonding	**Number**	**%**	**Number**	**%**
The degree of academic support you have received since entering your current program				
Very Dissatisfied	1	1.0	4	3.1
Dissatisfied	10	9.7	16	12.5
Somewhat Disatisfied	33	32.0	44	34.4
Satisfied	48	46.6	44	34.4
Very Satisfied	11	10.7	20	15.6
TOTAL*	**103**	**100**	**128**	**100**
The feeling that you are associated with people who are supportive of your professional goals				
Very Dissatisfied	2	1.9	5	3.8
Dissatisfied	11	10.7	22	16.8
Somewhat Disatisfied	31	30.1	33	25.2
Satisfied	44	42.7	47	35.9
Very Satisfied	15	14.6	24	18.3
TOTAL**	**103**	**100**	**131**	**100**

* Not significant at the .05 level

** Significant at the .05 level, with 4df

Table 24C

manner. Voicing some form of dissatisfaction were 24.6 percent of the non-McKnight students and only 10.7 percent of the McKnight Fellows. This finding was important because a peer networking system is an important aspect of the McKnight Model, and these data supported its existence.

The two groups were asked if they had an opportunity to meet other students with similar interests. No significant difference was found. However, 18.4 percent of non-McKnight students indicated dissatisfaction and only 1.7 percent of McKnight Fellows.

When McKnight Fellows and non-McKnight students were asked if they had "opportunities to bond with other students," a significant difference was found. Almost 90 percent of the McKnight Fellows indicated satisfaction, and only 74.3 percent of non-McKnight students indicated their satisfaction.

Again, data are revealed that support the McKnight Model. Bonding was felt to take place during the various conferences and meetings held for McKnight Fellows. Supporting evidence was revealed in Table 24.

McKnight Fellows and non-McKnight students were asked if anyone was available on campus to assist in resolving a campus problem. Both McKnight Fellows (84.5 percent) and non-McKnight students (77.7 percent) indicated satisfaction. However, the McKnight Fellows had the additional assistance from the FEF, which was not available for non-McKnight students.

Again, referring to Table 24, the two groups were asked to indicate how they felt about the psychological support received from their university. A significant difference was found between the two groups, with McKnight Fellows (82.4 percent) expressing satisfaction more so than non-McKnight students (73.8 percent). Actually, 10.8 percent of non-McKnight students stated they were very dissatisfied, while only one percent of the McKnight Fellows expressed the same sentiment.

McKnight Fellows and non-McKnight students were asked about the degree of academic support they had received from their university since entering their current program. No significant difference was found. However, a slightly higher percentage of non-McKnight students (15.6) than McKnight Fellows (12.6) expressed dissatisfaction.

Lastly, Table 24 reveals how the two groups felt that people associated with them at their university supported their professional goals. Overall, McKnight Fellows (87.4 percent) were satisfied more so than non-McKnight students (79.4 percent). This difference was significant.

These data presented in Table 24 indicate that McKnight Fellows were, on the whole, more satisfied with the support, networking and bonding they experienced at their university than the non-McKnight students. This is not to say that the non-McKnight students were not satisfied, just to point out that larger percentages of McKnight Fellows expressed feelings of satisfaction and in many cases higher levels of satisfaction.

Availability of Activities and Social Events

Table 25 reveals that a significant difference was not found between the two groups on how they felt about the availability of activities and social events at their university. Approximately 30 percent of the non-McKnight students and 28.4 percent of the McKnight Fellows expressed feelings of dissatisfaction. The high percent of dissatisfaction expressed by both groups could be indicative of some sense of social isolation. Earlier it was found that both McKnight Fellows and non-McKnight students shared information, worked on group projects and problem solved with other students from their university. Therefore, it seems that there was less academic isolation on these campuses.

Table 25:
Availability of Activities/Social Events to McKnight Fellows and Non-McKnight Students

Educational Characteristic	McKnight Fellows		Non-McKnight Students	
	Number	%	Number	%
The availability of activities/social events that meet with your interests				
Very Dissatisfied	8	7.8	10	7.8
Dissatisfied	21	20.6	29	22.5
Somewhat Disatisfied	37	36.3	47	36.4
Satisfied	29	28.4	33	25.6
Very Satisfied	7	6.9	10	7.8
TOTAL	**102**	**100**	**129**	**100**

X2 = .329 with 4df (Not significant at the .05 level)

Table 25

Attitudes Toward Academic Advising

Table 26 provides a breakdown of how effective the two groups felt academic advising was on their campus. Respondents were asked five questions, beginning with the level of advising displayed by their program advisor. Approximately 89 percent of the McKnight Fellows and 83.4 percent of the non-McKnight students expressed some degree of satisfaction in the interest shown by their advisor in their program. This difference was not significant.

The two groups were asked about the availability of their academic advisor when needed. Although not significant, a slightly higher percentage of McKnight Fellows (91.9) than non-McKnight students (87.1) were satisfied with the availability of their academic advisor.

Still referring to Table 26, 92.9 percent of the McKnight Fellows and 88.6 percent of the non-McKnight students felt satisfied that faculty in their program and their university were willing to provide assistance when needed. This difference was not significant.

Next, respondents were asked about the level of interaction they have had with faculty in their major area of study. Compared to the three previous questions just discussed, higher percentages of dissatisfaction were revealed by both groups. Almost 17 percent of the McKnight Fellows and 17.5 percent of the non-McKnight students stated they were dissatisfied with the level of interaction that had occurred between them and faculty in their major area of study. Again, no significant difference was found.

Last, McKnight Fellows and non-McKnight students were asked about the quality of the advice they had been provided while planning their program. Although not significant, a slight difference was found (see Table 26). More than 18 percent of the McKnight Fellows and 19.7 percent of the non-McKnight students indicated some level of dissatisfaction with the quality of advice received while planning their program.

These data shown in Table 26 provided some insight into the attitudes of McKnight Fellows and non-McKnight students concerning academic advising on their university campuses. Although significant differences were not found, slightly higher percentages of

Table 26:
Attitudes of McKnight Fellows and Non-McKnight Students Toward Academic Advising.

Attitudes Toward Current University	McKnight Fellows		Non-McKnight Students	
Academic Advising	**Number**	**%**	**Number**	**%**
The interest shown by your advisor in your academic program				
Very Dissatisfied	4	3.9	9	6.8
Dissatisfied	7	6.9	13	9.8
Somewhat Disatisfied	20	19.6	25	18.8
Satisfied	35	34.3	37	27.8
Very Satisfied	36	35.3	49	36.8
TOTAL*	**102**	**100**	**133**	**100**
The availability of your academic advisor to provide assistance when needed				
Very Dissatisfied	2	2.0	7	5.3
Dissatisfied	7	6.9	10	7.6
Somewhat Disatisfied	22	21.6	24	18.3
Satisfied	32	31.4	42	32.1
Very Satisfied	39	38.2	48	36.6
TOTAL*	**102**	**100**	**131**	**100**
The willingness of faculty to provide assistance when needed				
Very Dissatisfied	3	2.9	3	2.3
Dissatisfied	5	4.9	12	9.1
Somewhat Disatisfied	28	27.2	24	18.2
Satisfied	39	37.9	56	42.4
Very Satisfied	28	27.2	37	28.0
TOTAL*	**103**	**100**	**132**	**100**

Table 26A

Table 26 (cont):
Attitudes of McKnight Fellows and Non-McKnight Students Toward Academic Advising.

Attitudes Toward Current University	**McKnight Fellows**		**Non-McKnight Students**	
Academic Advising	**Number**	**%**	**Number**	**%**
The level of interaction you have had with faculty in your major area of study				
Very Dissatisfied	2	2.0	8	6.1
Dissatisfied	15	14.7	15	11.4
Somewhat Disatisfied	33	32.4	31	23.5
Satisfied	28	27.5	42	31.8
Very Satisfied	24	23.5	36	27.3
TOTAL*	**102**	**100**	**132**	**100**
The quality of advice provided you for planning your program				
Very Dissatisfied	6	5.8	8	6.1
Dissatisfied	13	12.6	18	13.6
Somewhat Disatisfied	32	31.1	34	25.8
Satisfied	35	34.0	43	32.6
Very Satisfied	17	16.5	29	22.0
TOTAL*	**103**	**100**	**132**	**100**

* Not significant at the .05 level

Table 26B

McKnight Fellows than non-McKnight students were satisfied with the level of academic advising received. Higher percentages of dissatisfaction were revealed by both groups concerning "interaction with faculty" and "advice in planning their program." One possible reason why McKnight Fellows displayed higher degrees of dissatisfaction related to advising, was the fact that they had been socialized into the graduate school culture. Thus, they were more attuned to what one should expect from their graduate education. For non-McKnight students, their dissatisfaction more than likely stemmed from a general disaffectation many minority students suffer while in graduate school (see Blackwell, 1985).

Role Model

Turning to Table 27, respondents in the two groups were asked if there was a person they considered their "role model." Almost 64 percent of the McKnight Fellows and 69.4 percent of the non-McKnight students stated they had a person who served as a role model for them. This difference was not significant.

Of those persons who had a role model, the greatest percentage of the McKnight Fellows (41.5) and non-McKnight students (24.7) stated their role model was a faculty member within their current department. For McKnight Fellows the next greatest percentage (21.5) stated their role model was a non-faculty person who is highly regarded in higher education, while the next greatest percentage (21.5) for non-McKnight students was "other." This difference was not significant.

Finally, the two groups were asked the racial/ethnic identity of their role model (see Table 27). For both non-McKnight students (79.6 percent) and McKnight Fellows (72.3 percent), the racial identity of the role model with the greatest percentage of corresponding responses was African American. Of the other role models identified, 18.3 percent of the non-McKnight students stated "White" as the racial identity of their role model, and 15.4 percent and 12.5 percent of the McKnight Fellows identified "White" and "other minority" respectively.

Table 27:
Person Considered as Role Model by McKnight Fellows and Non-McKnight Students

Educational Characteristic	McKnight Fellows		Non-McKnight Students	
Person Considered "Role Model"	**Number**	**%**	**Number**	**%**
For You:*				
Yes	65	63.7	93	69.4
No	37	36.3	41	30.6
TOTAL	**102**	**100**	**134**	**100**
If yes, is the person:				
a faculty member in your department?	27	41.5	23	24.7
a faculty member in another department?	7	10.8	13	14.0
an assigned advisor?	2	3.1	3	3.2
a faculty person from another university?	9	13.8	18	19.4
a non-faculty member highly regarded in higher education?	14	21.5	16	17.2
an other?	6	9	20	22
TOTAL	**65**	**100**	**93**	**100**
If yes, Role model is:				
African-American	47	72.3	74	79.6
White	10	15.4	17	18.3
Member of another minority group	8	12.3	2	2.1
TOTAL	**65**	**100**	**93**	**100**

* Not significant at the .05 level

** X2 = 6.688; with 2df (Significant at the .05 level)

Table 27

Mentor

McKnight Fellows and non-McKnight students were asked whether or not there was a person they considered as their mentor. Looking at Table 28, 70.6 percent of the McKnight Fellows and 50 percent of the non-McKnight students stated they had a mentor who had assisted them with their program. Although a percentage difference was found between the two groups, this difference was not significant.

Of those identified as having a mentor, a faculty member in their department was the overwhelming choice of both McKnight Fellows

(66.7 percent) and non-McKnight students (57 percent). Approximately 18 percent of the McKnight Fellows also identified a faculty member in another department as their mentor. For non-McKnight students, an equal percentage (12.7) identified "assigned advisor" and faculty person from another institution as their mentor. This difference was significant.

Table 28 revealed that the racial/ethnic identity of the mentor of non-McKnight students (54.4 percent) and McKnight Fellows (54.2 percent) was most likely to be White. Approximately 39 percent of the non-McKnight students and 31.9 percent of the McKnight Fellows stated their mentor was African American. The difference between the two groups was not significant.

Table 28:

Person Considered as Mentor by McKnight Fellows and Non-Mcknight Students.

Educational Characteristic	McKnight Fellows		Non-Mcknight Students	
Person Considered by You As Mentor	Number	%	Number	%
Who has assisted you in your program*				
Yes	72	70.6	79	59.0
No	30	29.4	55	41.0
TOTAL	**102**	**100**	**134**	**100**
If yes, is the mentor:**				
a faculty member in your department?	48	66.7	45	57.0
a Faculty member in another department?	13	18.1	6	7.6
an assigned advisor?	2	2.8	10	12.7
a faculty person from another university?	0	0	10	12.7
a non-faculty member highly regarded in higher education?	2	2.8	2	2.5
an other?	**7**	**9.7**	**6**	**7.6**
TOTAL	**72**	**100**	**79**	**100**
If yes, Role model is:*				
African-American	23	31.9	31	39.2
White	39	54.2	43	54.4
Member of another minority group	10	14.0	5	6.3
TOTAL	**72**	**100**	**79**	**100**

* Not significant at the .05 level

** Significant at the .01 level

Table 28

The data related to mentoring differed for both McKnight Fellows and non-McKnight students when compared to the data found for role models. Whereas, role models were overwhelmingly African American (see Table 27), Whites were more likely to serve as mentors for both groups. This difference can be explained in that the mentoring process is more likely to be carried out by a faculty member because of the close contact necessary for this process to take place. Role models, on the other hand, can be provided by others within and outside of the department or even the university. A close examination of Tables 27 and 28 support this contention. This is also a reflection of faculty makeup at the graduate level.

Institutional Quality

Attitudes Toward Program Quality

Program quality is important to any graduate student pursuing a doctoral degree. Program quality has an impact on both the ability of the student to receive a placement after graduation in a respectable institution and on the future productivity of the student. McKnight Fellows and non-McKnight students were queried about their attitudes toward the quality of the program in which they were currently enrolled.

Looking at Table 29, both groups were asked about the quality of program offerings in meeting their current academic needs. A significant difference was found between the McKnight fellows and the non-McKnight students. Slightly more than 95 percent of the non-McKnight students and 89.4 percent of the McKnight Fellows expressed some form of satisfaction with the quality of their program in meeting their academic needs. Approximately 26 percent of the non-McKnight students and 13.6 percent of the McKnight Fellows were very satisfied with the quality of their program.

Ninety-four percent of the non-McKnight students and 92.2 percent of the McKnight Fellows were satisfied with the quality of instruction provided in their current program. This difference was not significant.

Table 29:
Attitudes of McKnight Fellows and Non-McKnight Students Toward Program Quality

Attitudes Toward Current University	McKnight Fellows		Non-McKnight Students	
Program Quality	**Number**	**%**	**Number**	**%**
The quality of program offerings to meet your academic needs				
Very Dissatisfied	2	1.9	2	1.5
Dissatisfied	9	8.7	4	3.0
Somewhat Disatisfied	19	18.5	30	22.6
Satisfied	59	57.3	62	46.6
Very Satisfied	14	13.6	35	26.3
TOTAL**	**103**	**100**	**133**	**100**
The quality of instruction provided				
Very Dissatisfied	1	1.0	2	1.5
Dissatisfied	7	6.8	6	4.5
Somewhat Disatisfied	28	27.2	30	22.6
Satisfied	48	46.6	59	44.4
Very Satisfied	19	18.5	36	27.1
TOTAL*	**103**	**100**	**133**	**100**
The academic challenge provided in your program				
Very Dissatisfied	0	0	1	.8
Dissatisfied	8	7.8	5	3.8
Somewhat Disatisfied	12	11.7	23	17.3
Satisfied	56	54.4	51	38.3
Very Satisfied	27	26.2	53	39.8
TOTAL	**103**	**100**	**133**	**100**

* Not significant at the .05 level: with 4df3
* Significant at the .05 level: with 4df

Table 29

Lastly, Table 29 indicates whether or not both groups felt their program provided an academic challenge. Non-McKnight students (95.4 percent) and McKnight Fellows (92.2 percent) expressed feelings of satisfaction. Almost 40 percent of the non-McKnight students were very satisfied, and 26.2 percent of the McKnight Fellows revealed similar feelings. This difference was significant.

Housing Availability

The two groups were asked about the availability of good housing that was on or near their current campus. Table 30 provides the responses given by McKnight Fellows and non-McKnight students. Although not significant, McKnight Fellows were found to be slightly more satisfied than non-McKnight students.

Table 30:
McKnight Fellows and Non-McKnight Students and Their Perception of the Availability of Good Housing.

Educational Characteristic	McKnight Fellows		Non-McKnight Students	
	Number	%	Number	%
The availability of good housing on or near campus				
Very Dissatisfied	7	6.9	8	7.3
Dissatisfied	7	6.9	9	8.3
Somewhat Disatisfied	17	16.8	24	22.0
Satisfied	44	43.6	47	43.1
Very Satisfied	26	25.7	21	19.3
TOTAL	101	100	109	100

X2=1.841; with 4df (Not significant at the .05 level)

Table 30

Approximately 86 percent of the McKnight Fellows and 84.6 percent of the non-McKnight students expressed some level of satisfaction. But more importantly, 25.7 percent of the McKnight Fellows were very satisfied with the availability of good housing on or near campus, while only 19.3 percent of the non-McKnight students felt likewise.

It is important to point out that the availability of good housing is relative to one's ability to afford the cost. McKnight fellows, with a more firm financial base in many cases than non-McKnight students, might have been more satisfied because they were better able to afford the cost of housing on or near campus.

Position at Florida College or University

One of the objectives of the McKnight Black Doctoral Fellowship Program is to increase the pool of Black doctorates seeking positions in higher education. As the pool is increased, the intent is that many of these students who have studied in the State of Florida will remain and accept positions in public and private colleges and universities within the state.

Table 31:
Whether or Not McKnight Fellows and Non-McKnight Students Would Consider a Position at a Florida College/University After Graduation.

Educational Characteristic	McKnight Fellows		Non-McKnight Students	
	Number	%	Number	%
Position at Florida college/university after graduation, if salary is competitive				
Yes	84	82.2	113	85.6
Not sure	16	15.7	16	9.9
Definitely not	2	1.9	6	4.5
TOTAL	**102**	**100**	**135**	**100**

X^2 = 2.779; with 2df (Not significant at the .05 level)

Table 31

Table 31 shows that 82.4 percent of the McKnight Fellows and 85.6 percent of the non-McKnight students stated that they would consider a position at a Florida college or university if the salary was competitive. This difference was not significant. Granted that a slightly higher percentage of non-McKnight students than McKnight Fellows would consider a Florida position, only 1.9 percent of the McKnight Fellows gave a definite no as compared to 4.5 percent of the non-McKnight students.

Data not shown revealed that non-McKnight students were more likely to have been a resident of Florida when they entered their current doctoral program than McKnight Fellows. This finding coupled with the finding that many non-McKnight students worked full-time while pursuing the doctoral degree part-time, can be looked upon as an indication that non-McKnight students probably had more ties to Florida than McKnight Fellows prior to entering a doctoral degree program. This would then account for the slightly higher percentage of non-McKnight students who definitely stated they would consider a position in a Florida college or university after graduation.

Summary

In summary, this section has provided an analysis of data collected from mailed questionnaires the McKnight Fellows and the non-McKnight students were asked to complete. These data were designed to fulfill two purposes: 1) to test the McKnight Model and 2) to look at the quality of academic programs and support mechanisms provided by doctoral universities within the State of Florida as seen by McKnight Fellows and non-McKnight students.

Clearly differences were found between the two groups, with the McKnight Fellows being better supported financially, more likely to major in non-traditional academic fields for African Americans, more likely to attend professional meetings and network with other students, and having a stronger support system. Perceptions of the McKnight Fellows and non-McKnight students toward their current university revealed fewer differences between the two groups.

Although differences were found between the two groups in how they perceived their support mechanisms and the quality of their academic programs provided by their universities, even when McKnight Fellows revealed less dissatisfaction than non-McKnight students, dissatisfaction among McKnight students was greater than might have been expected. Given the McKnight model discussed and the literature reviewed, one would have to assume that the degree of dissatisfaction revealed by each group was for quite different reasons. These data clearly revealed that McKnight Fellows had a strong support system, received academic advice and were made aware of how the graduate school culture functioned. From the literature review, it is clear that most minority students became disassociated with their graduate program because of a lack of mentoring by faculty and a general feeling of isolation from faculty and majority students. Then, the question becomes: Why did McKnight Fellows display the degree of dissatisfaction that was revealed in this study? The most plausible explanation would seem to be the socialization McKnight Fellows received through the FEF in how graduate school culture functioned. In other words, McKnight Fellows, regardless of the external support provided by the FEF, were attuned to what to expect from their academic program and from their graduate peers. When their interaction and interpersonal relationship with faculty, advisors and other graduate students in their program was less than expected, the result was some degree of dissatisfaction.

6

Predictive Model for the Success of African-American and Other Minority Graduate Students

The objective of this evaluative study has been to develop a predictive model, based upon the McKnight Model, that can be used by colleges and universities to educate minority graduate students. While the emphasis of this research has been on African-American doctoral students, the proposed model is geared toward the education of minority students at both the master's and doctoral levels. Focus has been placed on the doctoral level because an important need has emerged in higher education that this research was designed to address. This need centers around the lack of production of minority doctorates, especially African-American and Hispanic doctorates, at a time when it is projected that traditional or majority faculty at American colleges and universities are due to decline. By the year 2000 substantial decreases are projected, primarily through retirement. Since these same demographic projections show that majority faculty will not be able to replace themselves, causing severe shortages among college and university faculties, it seems appropriate that the graduate education of minorities be addressed. Projections presented in this study have shown that while decreases in the White population are expected, minorities are expected to increase in number and as a proportion of the total American population.

Current research on doctoral and graduate education is somewhat sparse and research devoted to minorities is almost nonexistent. Despite the paucity of research to undergird policy formulation and programmatic planning, one national program has emerged that when compared with other current programs, reveals a definite edge in the education of African-American doctoral students (see Claque, 1990). The program being referred to is the McKnight Black Doctoral Fellowship Program and, thus, the focus of this study.

Testing the McKnight Model

Recruitment

The McKnight Model has overcome a traditional obstacle in the recruitment of African-American doctoral students in that it recruits nationally as opposed to most recruitment programs at colleges and universities. Traditional graduate programs are most likely to recruit on a local or regional level (Blackwell, 1987). These data showed that both McKnight Fellows and non-McKnight students were recruited nationally, based on where they received their undergraduate degree. Although not shown in the previous chapter, over 140 baccalaureate institutions located from Maine to California were identified as those attended by both groups. Also not shown, but important, was the fact that based on place of birth, which was used to determine urban-rural origins, McKnight Fellows were spread more nationally than non-McKnight students. Non-McKnight students tended to come from the southeastern part of the United States and Florida, more so than McKnight Fellows. Of course, for both McKnight Fellows and non-McKnight students, a disproportionately large number came from Florida. The MDF recruitment effort also accounts for many of the non-McKnight scholars getting into the applicant pool and subsequently matriculating.

Of interest, was the fact that a high proportion of McKnight Fellows and non-McKnight students were graduated from historically black colleges and universities (HBCU). This finding coupled with the success of the McKnight Fellows, as measured by grade point average, provides two points of interest. One is the assumption that in order to recruit graduate students who will be academically successful, recruitment emphasis should be on the top research universities in the country. Second is the more insidious, but related, assumption that somehow HBCU produce inferior or less prepared students. These data do not support either of these assumptions. Remember, one of the basic assumptions articulated during the discussion of the McKnight Model was that African-American doctoral students do not have to mirror the profile of the majority male doctoral student to be successful as it often has been assumed. Given the academic success of the McKnight Fellows, there were not significant differences between the undergraduate or master's level GPA between McKnight Fellows and non-McKnight students. These data dispel any notion that the success of the McKnight Black Doctoral Fellowship Program was due to the recruitment of academically superior students. Stated differently, these data clearly show that it is the outcome of the McKnight Model and not the academically talented student recruited as measured by GRE and GPA, that spells success. Approximately 37 percent of the McKnight Fellows had undergraduate GPAs of less than 3.00 and 19.6 percent had GPAs between 3.00 and 3.24. It is also important to reemphasize that a significantly larger percentage of the non-McKnight students when compared to McKnight Fellows had already received a graduate degree prior to entering their current doctoral program. Having completed a graduate degree provided proven evidence of their ability to do graduate work.

There are four other factors related to recruitment that are worthy of note. As was previously mentioned, decreases in the doctoral participation rate for African Americans have occurred over the last decade, with decreases being the most apparent among African-American males. Looking at these findings, non-McKnight students reflect gender differences, with a higher proportion of females over males. For McKnight Fellows, the trend was reversed, with a slightly higher proportion of males over females. The assumption that Black males are not available for graduate study has been challenged.

Two related factors in the profile of the students recruited by the MDF Program and those who were not, were the significant differences found in marital status and age. McKnight Fellows were of a younger age and less likely to be married than non-McKnight students. Both these factors might help account for what is a faster graduation rate for McKnight Fellows. Although not significant, higher percentages of non-McKnight students than McKnight Fellows were still enrolled in their programs seven years and beyond. Being relatively young and without immediate family obligations could possibly be a factor with regard to time to degree completion. Certainly, the lack of immediate family obligation, which can be a distraction, would be important.

Studies (Thomas, 1987; Clewell, 1987 and VANT and Associates, 1988) have pointed to the importance of middle-class status or a strong orientation toward middle-class values in graduate school success. These data clearly show that for both McKnight Fellows and non-McKnight students middle-class status was not predominant. More than 63 percent of the McKnight Fellows and 66.9 percent of non-McKnight students were from working- and lower-class backgrounds.

Student Support System

An important aspect of the McKnight Model is the support provided to the McKnight Fellows by the MDF Program. The establishment of campus liaison persons that help to provide support is a part of that system. McKnight Fellows have three alternatives to rely on for support and assistance: 1) the traditional avenue of faculty and/or faculty advisor, 2) the campus liaison person, and 3) program officials at the Florida Education Fund. The FEF calls this a concentric model of student support.

These data indicated that McKnight Fellows perceived they were getting more support and assistance on campus than expressed by non-McKnight students. Significantly more of the McKnight Fellows than the non-McKnight students were satisfied with the psychological support they received on campus. Again, in terms of academic support, a slightly higher proportion of McKnight Fellows over non-McKnight students expressed sentiments of satisfaction. Willie and Cunnigen (1981) point out the importance of a support system for Black students at majority colleges and universities. They further state that the first year of graduate school matriculation is the most stressful and often determines whether or not the student persists. Referring back to the McKnight Model, the orientation session for new students, the annual conference and the mid-year conference all provide important support during their first year as well as in subsequent years for McKnight Fellows.

Financial Support

Without a doubt, heretofore financial support has been found to be the most important single factor affecting whether or not African-American students complete graduate degrees (Blackwell, 1987; Upton and Pruitt, 1985; Scott, 1981; and Willie et al., 1991). Furthermore, African-American graduate students who are the most successful in completing their degrees are individuals who are receiving full financial support from the beginning to degree completion, including support for books and other incidentals (Willie et al., 1991 and Scott, 1981). The MDF Program, through negotiations with participating universities, provides full support for up to five years. With a funding level of $11,000 annually, the addition of tuition, books, health insurance, a computer allowance and travel support, McKnight Fellows are some of the best funded graduate students in the United States. Adequate funding is important because it allows the student to study full-time without the additional burden of a part-time or full-time job. Given normal progress toward graduation, the student is not concerned with funding sources year after year, for he or she knows it will be provided.

These data clearly revealed a significant difference in the funding level received by McKnight Fellows and that received by non-McKnight doctoral students. As was pointed out during the data analysis section, most McKnight Fellows received all their funding through the Florida Education Fund and those that did not receive any funding had moved into their fourth or fifth year of study and were receiving full funding from their university at the same level as provided previously by the Florida Education Fund.

Non-McKnight students, on the other hand, revealed substantially less institutional support than did McKnight Fellows. Higher proportions of non-McKnight students revealed savings and personal loans as their main source of funding. Most importantly, less than a combined 10 percent of the non-McKnight students received funding from university research assistantships, state fellowships, U.S. Government fellowships, non-McKnight private fellowships, veteran's benefits, or parents. Supported is Upton and Pruitt's (1985) suggestion that financial aid be separated between minority and non-minority students and specifically designed for African-American students. Obviously, based on these findings, African-American doctoral students do not fare well in the distribution of financial assistance. Although these data are based on Florida universities, there is no reason to assume things are better in other public or private institutions (see Upton and Pruitt, 1985).

Willie et al. (1991) state that one of the major reasons why African-American doctoral students do not complete their degrees is that they are only financially supported for the first three years, but not for year four or five. Private sources such as the Lilly Endowment which, along with the United Negro College Fund, sponsored the Lilly/UNCF Faculty Development Program that Willie et al. studied, provided funding for up to three years. Willie et al. found that many of those who participated in the program were not able to finish in three years and did not complete their doctoral degrees. As a result of their research, Willie et al. called for doctoral granting institutions to provide financial support that will continue for up to five years of study. Findings from Willie et al. provide additional support to the McKnight Model that provides for up to five years of support: three years by the Florida Education Fund and two years by participating institutions.

Role Modeling/Mentoring/Bonding/Networking

As was stated earlier, McKnight Fellows are introduced to the graduate school culture at the beginning of their first year of matriculation at the McKnight orientation workshop for new students which occurs over a full weekend or three-day period. A socialization process continues throughout their first year of study with the Annual Fellows Conference and the mid-year conference, and this process is repeated as long as they are McKnight Fellows (includes year four and five). This type of support system addresses socialization, role modeling, mentoring, bonding and networking.

Both McKnight fellows and non-McKnight students were generally satisfied with the assistance they received on campus in solving campus problems, concern displayed by faculty in their academic progress and the academic support they had received while on campus.

These findings support the McKnight Model in that evidence was presented that bonding took place at conferences and workshops and the establishment of a peer support network was more likely to take place among McKnight Fellows than non-McKnight students. Significant differences were also found between the two groups in terms of support of professional goals and psychological support. In both these areas of support, McKnight Fellows were more likely to be satisfied and experienced a higher degree of satisfaction than non-McKnight students.

These data support the earlier findings of Willie and Cunnigen (1981) and Willie (1987) that emphasize the importance of mentoring and sponsoring as well as teaching and advising. Not fully supported were the findings of Levinson (1978) who stated that women and minorities have problems finding mentors. More than 70 percent of the McKnight Fellows stated they had a mentor, and the mentor was most likely to be a faculty member from their department. Non-McKnight students had similar experiences, but to a lesser degree.

Most revealing was the fact that for both McKnight Fellows and non-McKnight students their mentor was most likely to be White. African-American mentors were a distant second. This is explained clearly by the lack of diversity among graduate faculties.

Role models revealed a different set of circumstances. A high proportion of both groups stated they had a role model, and almost twice the proportion of McKnight fellows over non-McKnight students stated their role model was a faculty member from their department. For McKnight fellows, the next most likely response was that their role models were a non-faculty person who is highly regarded in higher education. Role models differed from mentors in that for both groups role models were most likely to be African American. Majority role models were a very distant second for both groups.

Further shown was that for both groups, when professors assigned group projects, McKnight Fellows and non-McKnight students were assigned to mixed groups. Both McKnight Fellows and non-McKnight students shared information with other students at their current university and at other Florida universities. McKnight Fellows were more likely than non-McKnight fellows to share information with students at other Florida universities.

Role modeling, mentoring, bonding and networking are not simplistic processes, but operate at many different levels. These data showed that the mentoring process was more likely to occur within one's own department because of the propinquity of the faculty member to the student. Although the MDF Program provides mentors through their Council of Elders, who are senior level university faculty and administrators who can be contacted for support and/or assistance, these data indicated that members of the Council of Elders were most likely perceived by McKnight Fellows as role models. The higher proportion of majority mentors over African-American mentors, of course, was partly a function of the paucity of African-American faculty present on the campuses of Florida universities. This would be especially true for McKnight Fellows who were not pursuing degrees in education and had a disproportionately large number, relative to other programs nationally, who were in the natural sciences, computer sciences, engineering, health sciences and business. Since these are non-traditional fields for African Americans, there were few African-American faculty present. On the other hand, it is noteworthy that majority faculty were available and were perceived by McKnight Fellows and non-McKnight students as mentors.

Opportunities to bond and network with other students were available to McKnight Fellows more so than non-McKnight students because of two factors. One factor was the conferences and workshops provided by the MDF Program. The second factor was the greater opportunity to attend professional conferences as revealed by the McKnight Fellows over the non-McKnight students. The importance of the accessibility to other McKnight Fellows matriculating at universities throughout Florida for McKnight Fellows over non-McKnight students cannot be overemphasized. The sense of isolation often felt by many minority students at majority institutions is an important factor in whether or not they are successful academically (see Fleming, 1984). Bonding and networking with other students and with the Council of Elders, who were perceived as role models, is an important facet of the McKnight Model. The orientation for new students, the annual conference, and the mid-year conference all served to help McKnight Fellows adjust to the social and academic climate of majority colleges and universities. Fleming (1984), in her book *Blacks in College*, maintained that majority institutions often downplay the need for adjustment, which is extremely important when students are moving from predominantly Black institutions to majority institutions. The socialization and adjustment process undertaken by the MDF Program is important to the success of its participants.

Summary

These data and findings from other studies support the McKnight Model and its impact on the graduate education of African Americans. When compared with non-McKnight students matriculating in graduate programs in Florida, McKnight Fellows revealed significant differences in the important areas of recruitment, financial support, role models, attendance at conferences/meetings and networking/ bonding and support systems. Each of these areas are germane to the success of the McKnight Model.

7

McKnight Graduates and Candidates

In Chapter 2, a review of the literature revealed that throughout higher education it was generally agreed that more effective strategies were needed to recruit and retain minorities in post-secondary educational institutions. While baccalaureate degree granting institutions serve as a pipeline into graduate education and, therefore, need to improve their recruitment and retention strategies, new and more effective mechanisms are acutely needed at the graduate level. Earlier it was shown that the number of African Americans awarded doctorate degrees between 1977, the year most degrees were awarded, and 1991 has decreased. Although an increase was registered between 1987, the year the fewest degrees were awarded since 1977, and 1991, the awarding of doctorate degrees nationally to African Americans had not returned to the 1977 level.

These national data make it clear that the problem confronting graduate education in the United States is not only recruitment, but retention to graduation. Compelling evidence was presented by Willie, et. al. (1991) showing that the level of support provided African-American doctoral students during their first year of graduate study favors recruitment over retention. In many cases, financial support provided extends for a period not exceeding three years. Thus, many African-American doctoral students leave their graduate institutions without finishing, and never return to complete their degree. Evidence presented in this study thus far indicated that the single most important factor influencing whether or not African-American doctoral students complete their degree is financial support. The importance of financial support was shown in the literature review and in comparing McKnight Black Doctoral students with non-McKnight Black Doctoral students.

The McKnight Model is offered in this evaluative study as one that provides viable strategies not only in the recruitment of African American and other minority students into doctoral programs, but also in the retention of these students to graduation. The McKnight Model was presented in detail in Chapter 4. Chapter 5 compared McKnight Fellows with non-McKnight African-American students enrolled at doctoral degree granting institutions in Florida. These data clearly showed differences between McKnight Fellows and non-McKnight students as they matriculated in their doctoral programs and thus, provided a partial test of the validity of the McKnight Model.

To complete the test of the McKnight Model, it is necessary to examine those individuals who have completed their doctoral degrees and those who have advanced to candidacy. Candidacy is operationally defined here as those students who have completed their course requirements and who have successfully completed their comprehensive examination.

As of the end of 1993, 148 McKnight Fellows were enrolled in doctoral programs, including the 35 who have advanced to candidacy. An additional 56 McKnight Fellows have received their doctoral degrees. The focus of this chapter will be to look at the McKnight Fellows who have received their doctorates and those who have advanced to candidacy, with the primary emphasis being placed on the former. By providing an analysis of those students who have finished their degree or who have advanced to candidacy, a more complete test of the McKnight Model can be provided.

It should be pointed out that these data used in looking at graduates and candidates were collected in October, 1993. Therefore, some of those who were candidates then have now completed their degree. Additionally, some students have reached the candidacy stage since these data were collected. Because of these changes in status, differences will be apparent between the number of graduates as of the end of 1993 and when these data were collected.

These data were collected by telephone interview. The staff at the Florida Endowment Fund contacted each McKnight Fellow who had completed their degree and who had advanced to candidacy as of October, 1993. Looking at Table 32 below, it can be seen that a total of 83 of the McKnight Fellows had either completed their doctorate degree or had advanced to candidacy. Broken down, 54.2 percent or 45 had graduated and 45.8 percent or 38 had advanced to candidacy. Of these data presented, a more complete analysis will be provided of the graduates than the candidates. The reason obviously is that the primary objective here is to determine if traditionally cited factors such as educational background (parent and family members, type of college graduated from, and demographic variables) and performance criteria prior to entering doctoral programs (GRE scores, GPA, etc.) are the primary criteria in determining whether or not a student graduates. If it can be shown that these factors did not have undue influence, then certain assumptions made earlier about the McKnight Model gain strength.

Data presented in Chapter 5 revealed that the success of the McKnight Black Doctoral Fellowship Program (MDF) was due to the McKnight Model, not the recruitment of academically superior students. The McKnight Model included a retention process, that in addition to providing financial support for five years, provided a support system for its students that drew upon role models, mentors, bonding and networking. Equally important to the McKnight support system was the role the McKnight staff played in assisting students who faced personal problems or problems at their matriculating institutions.

Table 32:
Number and Percent of Graduates and Candidates

Status	Number	%
Graduates	45	54.2
Candidates	38	45.8
Total	83	100

X2 = .604 with 1df, not significant at the .05 level. This number represents McKnight Fellows who were interviewed as of October 1993. It was not possible to interview all graduates and candidates at that time. Since that time, additional McKnight Fellows have graduated and others have moved to candidacy.

Demographic Characteristics

Gender

In Chapter 5 it was revealed that of the total number of McKnight Fellows who responded to the original survey, 51.5 percent were male and 48.5 percent were female. The survey of graduates and candidates (see Table 33) revealed that of those who have been retained to graduation, 66.7 percent were female and 33.3 percent were male. Gender differences between candidates were not as apparent, but differences existed between the females (58.3 percent) and the males (41.7 percent).

Through the use of their recruitment mechanisms, the MDF Program is clearly addressing the need to increase the number of African-American doctorates. Most importantly, as it was brought out earlier, the recruitment success of this program goes against the national trends of African-American females at the doctoral level outnumbering African-American males. This national trend has been evident since 1977. McKnight recruitment efforts showed no significant gender differences.

Table 33:
Number and Percent of Graduates and Candidates by Gender

Gender	Graduate		Candidate	
	Number	Percent	Number	Percent
Female	30	66.7	21	58.3
Male	15	33.3	15	41.7
Total	45	100	36	100

X2 = .619 with 1df, not significant at .05

Given the graduation and candidacy data presented in this study, it would have to be concluded that the McKnight Model is successful both in terms of recruitment and graduation. Although gender differences did not exist based on recruitment, retention to graduation revealed differences, but they were not significant.

Age

Looking at Table 34, it can be clearly seen that these data on age do not reflect traditional characteristics. Within the last few years nationally, the trend has moved more toward older nontraditional students at both the undergraduate and graduate levels.

In Chapter 5 it was revealed that 42.7 percent of the McKnight Fellows were under 30 years of age. It is interesting to note that 45.5 percent of the graduates and 47.3 percent of the candidates were under the age of 35. Approximately 16 percent of the graduates and 30.6 percent of the candidates were under the age of 30, and probably fell within what would be referred to as traditional age doctoral students.

Table 34:
Number and Percent of Graduates and Candidates by Age

Age	Graduate		Candidate	
	Number	Percent	Number	Percent
56 to 60	1	2.3	1	2.8
51 to 55	2	4.5	2	5.6
46 to 50	2	4.5	2	5.6
41 to 45	10	22.7	7	19.4
36 to 40	9	20.5	7	19.4
31 to 35	13	29.6	6	16.7
26 to 30	7	15.9	11	30.6
Total	44	100	36	100.1

X2 was not computed because of the low values in many of the cells Table 34

One of the questions that is often asked of older graduate students, and one that older students ask themselves is: "Given the production and employment years remaining, is the time spent in a doctoral program one that will pay off financially and in terms of accomplishments?" While the answer to this question would probably vary among individuals, and is really a personal response, older individuals are actually completing doctoral degrees. For the McKnight Fellows, 11.3 percent of the graduates and 14 percent of the candidates were over the age of 46. Considering the fact that the first doctoral degree awarded a McKnight Fellow was in 1988, this datum takes on added significance.

Wide variations in age are important to examine in the analysis of a model that is predicated on a strong system of social support. The McKnight Model is dedicated to providing an opportunity for its participants to socialize, motivate, and assist each other through a system of bonding and networking with one another as well as with African-American scholars who serve as role models. These data indicate that age is not an inhibiting factor in the success of McKnight Fellows. The model works for the young and old doctoral students as well.

Marital Status

There are two important factors that are related to marital status and graduate study. One is that having a family could possibly put additional pressure on academic obligations, since being married carries certain responsibilities as well. Second, the academic obligations required of a student matriculating in a doctoral program could put an additional strain on marital relationships.

Table 35:
Number and Percent of Graduates by Marital Status

Marital Status	Start of Program		End of Program	
	Number	Percent	Number	Percent
Single	17	48.6	15	42.9
Married	16	45.7	18	51.4
Divorced	2	5.7	2	5.7
Total	35	100	35	100

X2 = .244 with 2df, not significant at .05 level

McKnight graduates were asked about their marital status at the beginning of their doctoral program and when they completed their degree. By looking at Table 35, one can readily observe that two fewer students were single and two additional students were married between the time they began their program and when they graduated.

This change in marital status was due to the marriage of two McKnight Fellows during their graduate study. The fact that significant differences did not exist between the start of the program and the time of completion, particularly in terms of the 51.4 percent of the students who were married, seems to indicate that family obligations and academic responsibilities were manageable.

Children

Factors associated with working on a doctorate degree and being married can be magnified when children are involved. For single parents with children, pursuing a graduate degree could be an even more arduous process. Of the McKnight Fellows who had graduated, 40 percent or 14 had children (see Table 36). Closely examining the 14 who had children, it was found that 13 were married and one was divorced. Therefore, 13 of the 18 who were married at the completion of their degree had gone through at least part of the program while married with at least one child.[1]

Table 36:
Number and Percent of Graduates by Whether or Not They Have Children

Children	Number	Percentage
Yes	14	40
No	21	60
Total	35	100

X2 = 1.4 with 1df, not significant at .05 level

Educational Background of Family

Table 37 reveals the highest level of education that was completed by an immediate family member (the family that they grew up in) of the McKnight Fellows who had completed their degrees. Sixty percent of the graduates indicated that at least one member of their immediate family had completed between 16 to 17 years of education, which normally means having completed at least four years of post-high school education. Twenty percent indicated that at least one immediate family member had post-baccalaureate training, and only 2.9 percent or one graduate indicated the highest grade completed by an immediate family member was less than high school.

Table 37:
Number and Percent of Graduates by Highest Level of Education Achieved in the Family

Years of Education Achieved	Number	Percentage
20 to 21	4	11.4
18 to 19	3	8.6
16 to 17	'21	60
14 to 15	2	5.7
12 to 13	4	11.4
10 to 11	1	2.9
Total	35	100

X2 = were not completed because of the number of low values in the cells

First to Receive Graduate Degree

Middle-class status has traditionally been looked at as one criterion that has a positive impact on performance at the undergraduate and graduate level. Table 37 showed that at least 80 percent of the graduates indicated that at least one member of their immediate family had completed 16 or more years of education. Allen (1984) maintained that minority students from families that have records of educational achievement seem to pose less of an academic risk than those who are from families who lack a background of educational achievement.

Looking at Table 38, it can be seen that 62.9 percent of the graduates stated that they were not the first in their immediate family to receive a graduate degree. Of the 37.1 percent who stated they were the first to receive a graduate degree, approximately one-half came from families who had completed at least 16 years of education (see Table 37). Clearly the McKnight graduates were from families who had achieved some educational success.

Table 38:
Number and Percent of Graduates by First in Family to Receive Graduate Degree

First in the Family to Receive Graduate Degree	Number	Percentage
Yes	13	37.1
No	22	62.9
Total	35	100

X2 = 2.31 with 1df, not significant at .05 level

Educational Characteristics of McKnight Fellows

Baccalaureate Degree in Field of Study

Table 39 reveals whether or not McKnight Fellows who had graduated or who were candidates had obtained a bachelor's degree in their current field of study. Graduates (61.4) and candidates (63.9) were almost identical in the percentages who had bachelor's degrees in their current field of study.

Although a higher percentage in both groups had degrees in their current field of study, not having an undergraduate degree in the same field did not seem to make a difference. Therefore, the success of the McKnight Fellows seems to be attributable to factors other than an undergraduate degree in their current field of study.

Table 39:
Number and Percent of Graduates and Candidates by Baccalaureate in Field of Current Study

Bacculaureate in Field	Graduate		Candidate	
	Number	Percent	Number	Percent
Yes	27	61.4	23	63.9
No	17	38.6	13	36.1
Total	44	100	36	100

X2 = .054 with 1df, not significant at .05 level

Table 40:
Number and Percent of Graduates and Candidates by Master's Degree in the Field of Study

Master's in Fiels	Graduate		Candidate	
	Number	Percent	Number	Percent
Yes	31	70.5	19	52.8
No	13	29.5	17	47.2
Total	44	100	36	100

X2 = 2.64 with 1 df, not significant at .05 level

Master's Degree in Field of Study

Table 40 (above) presents data that looks at whether or not McKnight Fellows had a master's degree in their current field of study. For the graduates, 70.5 percent had master's in the same field of study. Candidates were more closely divided between those who had master's in the same field (52.8 percent) and those who did not (47.2 percent). As with baccalaureate degrees, whether or not McKnight Fellows had a master's degree in their current field of study seems to make little difference.

Undergraduate Institution Attended

Looking at Table 41, it can be determined that whether or not McKnight Fellows attended a historically black college or university (HBCU) or a predominantly White institution for their undergraduate degree had little or no influence on their performance at the doctoral degree level. Exactly 50 percent of the graduates had attended HBCUs and predominantly White institutions. Although 61.1 percent of the candidates had attended predominantly white institutions and 38.9 percent had attended HBCUs, the difference was not significant.

Table 41:
Number and Percent of Graduates and Candidates by Type of Institution Received Baccalaureate Degree

Type of Institution	Graduate		Candidate	
	Number	Percent	Number	Percent
Historically Black	22	50	14	38.9
Predominantly White	22	50	22	61.1
Total	44	100	36	100

X2 = .98 with 1df, not significant at the .05 level

In Chapter 5 it was pointed out that McKnight Fellows had attended a wide range of HBCUs. Named were some of the more prestigious institutions like Morehouse College, Spelman College, Florida A and

M University, and Hampton University and some of the lesser known institutions such as Paine College, Benedict College, and Edward Waters College. It is important to keep in mind that integration has had a dysfunctional impact on the ability of HBCUs to attract the top African-American student. Although this state-of-affairs has changed in recent years, in the early years of integration HBCUs were left with having to educate graduate school administrators at predominantly White institutions who perceived HBCUs as lacking academically. Many predominantly White doctoral degree granting institutions still view graduates from HBCUs as being less well prepared for graduate study than African-American graduates from White institutions. These views have persisted despite more aggressive recruiting and attractive financial packages offered by HBCUs, like Florida A and M University, that have brought some of the top African-American students to campus. And HBCUs like Morehouse, Spelman, and Hampton, to name a few, have been inundated with applications from many of the top African-American high school graduates, as these graduates have responded to a move toward cultural pluralism and have attempted to escape the perceived racist label associated with predominantly White institutions.

These data indicate that the graduation and retention rates of McKnight Fellows are not tied to the type of institution from which they graduated. In other words, whether or not McKnight Fellows graduated from HBCUs or predominantly White institutions seems not to be a major factor influencing the graduation rates of African-American doctoral students.

Graduate Record Examination Scores (GRE)

The one factor that has traditionally been, and continues to be, considered as the best predictor of success in graduate school, is GRE scores. Many African-American educators and others in higher education have contended that GRE scores, while certainly one of the many factors to be considered in predicting the success of students from economically disadvantaged backgrounds, are certainly not *the* sole indicator of success. Graduate school admission officers often cite unacceptable GRE scores as the reason for low minority student applicant pools. What these officers are saying is that many minority students do not score at levels equal to or greater than arbitrarily determined scores (VANT, 1988; Blackwell, 1988).

Table 42:
Number and Percent of Graduates and Candidates by Total Graduate Record Examination Score

Age	Graduate		Candidate	
	Number	Percent	Number	Percent
1350 or >	1	2.5	-	-
1250 to 1349	2	5	1	3.2
1150 to 1249	5	12.5	1	3.2
1050 to 1149	7	17.5	9	29
950 to 1049	2	5	11	35.5
850 to 949	8	20	6	19.4
750 to 849	11	27.5	1	3.2
650 to 749	3	7.5	2	6.5
550 to 649	1	2.5	-	-
Total	40	100	31	100

Table 42 reveals data that raises strong concerns about traditional assumptions related to using GRE scores as single predictors of success in graduate education. Interestingly, one McKnight graduate had a total GRE score of between 550 and 649. Approximately 38 percent of the graduates and 9.7 percent of the candidates scored below 850 on the GRE. Slightly more than 57 percent of the graduates and 29.1 percent of the candidates scored less than 950.

Based on these data, it can be concluded that GRE scores, while important as one of the many indicators of graduate school success, is *not* the one predictor of success that many have assumed.

Grade Point Average (GPA)

Since both graduates and candidates have completed their course work, the final grade point average (GPA) for both groups is provided in Table 43. Approximately 23.7 percent of the graduates and 28.9 percent of the candidates indicated that they had a GPA of between 3.75 and 4.00 on a 4.00 point scale. Slightly more than 71 percent of the graduates had GPAs of 3.50 or greater, while 73.6 percent of the candidates indicated likewise.

Table 43:
Number and Percent of Graduates and Candidates by Final Grade Point Average (GPA)

Final GPA	Graduate		Candidate	
	Number	Percent	Number	Percent
4.0 to 3.75	9	23.7	11	28.9
3.74to 3.50	18	47.4	17	44.7
3.49 to 3.25	9	23.7	8	21.1
3.24 to 3.00	2	5.3	2	5.3
Total	38	100.1	38	100

To further explore the importance of the Graduate Record Examination as a predictor of success in graduate school, Table 44 compares the GPAs of both graduates and candidates with GRE scores. A close look at Table 44 shows that 55.9 percent or 10 of the McKnight Fellows with GPAs between 3.75 and 4.00 had scored less than 950 on the GRE. One student with a GPA between 3.75 and 4.00 had scored between 650 and 749 on the GRE. Individuals scoring this low are usually rejected for admission. Of the McKnight Fellows who had GPAs between 3.50 and 3.74, 50.2 percent scored less than 950 on the

GRE, with one student having scored between 550 and 659 on the GRE. Conversely, one of the students who scored high on the GRE had a GPA of between 3.00 and 3.24, which was the lowest category presented.

Table 44:
Number and Percent of Graduates and Candidates by Total GRE Score and Final GPA

Total GRE	Final Grade Point Average							
	4.00 to 3.75		3.74 to 3.50		3.49 to 3.25		3.24 to 3.00	
	#	%	#	%	#	%	#	%
1350 or Greater	1	5.6	-	-	-	-	-	-
1250 to 1349	-	-	1	3.3	-	-	1	20
1150 to 1249	2	11.1	1	3.3	2	18.2	-	-
1050 to 1149	1	5.6	6	20	4	36.4	2	40
950 to 1049	4	22.2	7	23.3	2	18.2	1	20
850 to 949	5	27.8	7	23.3	-	-	1	20
750 to 849	4	22.2	5	16.9	1	9	-	-
650 to 749	1	5.6	2	6.7	2	18.2	-	-
550 to 659	-	-	1	3.3	-	-	-	-
	18	100.1	30	100.1	11	100	5	100

The number of graduates and candidates had to be combined because of the low n's in the cells.

These data further substantiate the danger of an over-dependency on the GRE when predicting the success of African-American students in graduate school. This is one of the reasons the MDF Program does not require a specific GRE score as a criterion for eligibility to receive a scholarship. Florida state universities, which require a total GRE score of 1,000 as a threshold would not have admitted many of the McKnight Fellows who are graduating and who have reached the candidacy stage. However, through their partnership with the MDF Program, these students were admitted and, as these data indicated, were very successful.

Demand for Graduates

Number of Job Offers Received

One of the measures of the success of a program is the demand for its graduates. McKnight Fellows who had received their doctorate degrees were asked to provide the number of employment offers they received prior to accepting their first job after graduation, including post-doctoral positions. Table 45 indicates that 31.4 percent of the graduates received three employment offers and one graduate received eight offers. Receiving three or more offers were 65.8 percent of the graduates. Two recent graduates indicated that they had not received any employment offers at the time the survey was conducted.

Table 45:
Number and Percent of Graduates by Number of Job Offers Received.

Job Offers Received	Number	%
8	1	2.9
7	3	8.6
6	1	2.9
5	4	11.4
4	3	8.6
3	11	31.4
2	6	17.1
1	4	11.4
0	2	5.7
Total	35	100

Summary

This chapter serves to complement Chapter 5. While Chapter 5 provides a comparative analysis between McKnight and non-McKnight doctoral students studying at Florida universities, this chapter examined those McKnight Fellows who had graduated and those who were candidates for graduation. Chapter 5 revealed that differences existed between McKnight Fellows and non-McKnight students in terms of financial support, fields of study (non-McKnight students in significant numbers majored in education), exposure to professional meetings/conferences, the ability to network with other graduate students and having a support system.

This chapter provided the final test of the McKnight Model; the ability to move students to graduation. These data clearly reveal that the McKnight Model works, in that it is an effective mechanism for graduating minority and other financially disadvantaged graduate students. Show are that many of the traditional assumptions such as an overriding value placed on GRE scores and the devaluing of graduates from historically Black colleges and universities does not hold true. Graduate and candidate students in this study came to their graduate programs with GRE scores ranging from a high of 1350 to a low of 550. Even when GRE scores were compared with grade point averages, significant differences were not found. When graduates and candidates of predominantly White colleges and universities were compared with those from historically Black colleges and universities, no significant differences were found.

As we move into the 21st Century, it is going to be essential that America provide educational opportunities for all of her citizens from kindergarten through graduate school. Granted, all Americans will not attend graduate school, but it will be necessary for graduate schools to move away from the paradigm that has traditionally favored the white male student with the highest GRE scores and those who have graduated from predominantly White colleges and universities. This study has clearly shown that one other model "the McKnight Model" should be given serious consideration in the education of non-traditional graduate students.

Epilogue

You can not build a house for last year's summer
—African Proverb

It was our great fortune that the McKnight Doctoral Fellowship Program began during a period when the connection between desegregating American higher education and the visible lack of participation of people of color could no longer be ignored. We say fortuitous because a major foundation, which made approximately 95 percent of its gifts in only one state, decided to find projects beyond its traditional giving area. Then a man in the leadership position at the foundation and a woman in a leadership position in the Florida state university system were both sensitive to the challenge and committed to the proposition that change was possible. All of these forces converging on the real proposition—which was how do you desegregate American higher education?—was indeed fortuitous.

After many years of exposure, one can conclude that the only way you desegregate American higher education is to produce as many Ph.D.s as quickly as possible. The academy must be made to understand that these new Ph.D.s need not be "superstars" but rather ordinary, everyday faculty members, like most of the academy! The title of this manuscript should be illustrative. It should say to all that "ordinary" people who are committed and willing to work hard to accomplish an important goal—with the proper support and financial stability—can achieve great things.

There are a number of matters that need to be explored further in discussing the connection between producing more Ph.D.s and the status of the historically disadvantaged in American society. The first issue that must be tackled and is also prominently mentioned in the volume *In Pursuit of the Ph.D.*, by Bowen and Rudenstine (1992), is that we must provide better data about this segment of American higher education.

Second, should doctoral level education continue to be unaccountable? Institutions and graduate faculty ought to have a responsibility to see that students who get to the ABD (all but the dissertation) stage actually complete the requirements. So we need a process of systematic follow-up. Also, we must understand that all of this is in the best interest of developing America's human resources. These students have toiled anywhere from five to ten years to complete a doctoral degree. They should not be left negotiating all by themselves. Those who are most successful at the doctoral level usually point to a mentor, a major professor, or a dissertation committee chair who was very instrumental in guiding them through the rocky terrain of graduate school. Letting so much talent fall through the cracks, after such heavy personal and financial investment, is irresponsible.

Third, it is necessary that additional efforts to increase the number of minority Ph.D.s as quickly as possible be encouraged: in all states, with regional compacts, and through quasi-public entities.

The global village of the 21st century is going to require that America use more effectively all of its available human resources. In order to remain competitive in this new global environment, it is going to take new thinking from new perspectives that will, in fact, address the major challenges of the new world social order.

Bibliography

A Difference of Degrees: State Initiative to Improve Minority Student Achievement. State Higher Education Officers (SHEEO), 1987.

Abatso, Yvonne (1987). "Coping Stratagies: Retaining Black Students in College." In Anne S. Pruitt (Ed.) *In Pursuit of Equality in Higher Education* (pp 123-131) Dix Hills, N.J.: General Hall.

Adams, H.G. (1986, October). *Minority Participation in Graduate Education: An Action Plan.* The Report of the National Invitational Forum on the Status of Minority Participation in Graduate Education. (Conference Proceedings No. 021, 15pp). Proceedings of the National Invitational Forum on the Status of Minority Participation in Graduate Education. Notre Dame, IN: National Consortium for Grad. Degrees for Minorities in Engineering, Inc.

Adams, H.G. (1988). "Tommorrow's Professorate: Insuring Minority Participation Through Talent Development Today." Paper presented at the Engineering Dean's Council Student Education, Washington, D.C.

Allen, Walter R., et al. (1982). *Winter 1981 Study of Black_Graduate/ Professional Students Attending Predominately, State-Supported Universities*. (Preliminary report, No. 143,16pp.). Ann Arbor, MI: University of Michigan,Center for Afro-American and African Studies.

Allen, Walter R., et al. (1984). *Graduate Professional Survey*, National Study of Black College Students. Preliminary report: 1982. (Report No. 141, 24pp.). Ann Arbor, MI: University of Michigan, Center for Afro-American and African Studies.

Allen, Walter R., (1986). "Correlates of Black Student Adjustment, Achievement, and Aspirations at a Predominantly White Southern University." In Gail E. Thomas (Ed.). *Black Students in Higher Education* (pp.126-141). Westport, CT: Greenwood Press.

Allen, Walter R., (1987). "How To Improve the College Experience for Black Students." *Change* Magazine (May/June).

American Council on Education (ACE), Office of Minorities in Higher Education, 1992. Eleventh Annual Status Report, Deborah J. Carter and Reginald Wilson, 1992.

Astin, Alexander W., (1982). *Minorities in American Higher Education*. San Francisco: Jossey-Bass.

Astin, Helen S. and Patricia Cross, (1981). "Black Students in Black and White Institutions." In Gail E. Thomas (Ed.). *Black Students in Higher Education* (pp. 30-45). Dix Hill, NY: General Hall.

Avakian, A.N. (1982). "Race and Sex Differences in Student Retention at an Urban University." *College and University*, 57 (Winter): 160-165.

Becker, Howard (1970). "The Struggles for Power on Campus." In Howard Becker (ed), *Campus Power Struggle.* Chicago: Transaction Books.

Blackwell, James E., (1981). *Mainstreaming Outsiders: The Production of Black Professionals.* 1st Edition Bayside: General Hall.

Blackwell, James E. (1983). *Networking and Mentoring: A Study of Crossgenerational Experiences of Blacks in Graduate and Professional Schools.* Atlanta: Southern Education Foundation.

Blackwell, James E. (1984). *Desegregation of State Systems of Higher Education: An Assessment.* Atlanta, Ga.: Southern Education Foundation.

Blackwell, James E. (1988). "Faculty Issues: The Impact on Minorities." *The Review of Higher Education* (Summer): 417-434.

Blackwell, James E. (1987). *Mainstreaming Outsiders: The Production of Black Professionals.* 2nd. Edition Dix Hills, N.Y.: General Hall.

Boyd, W.M. (1977, Summer). "Black Undergraduates Succeed in White Colleges." *Educational Record*, 58, 309-315.

Boyer, Ernest L. (1983). *High School: A Report on Secondary Education in America.* New York: Harper and Row.

Borkowski, Francis T. (1988). "The University President's Role in Establishing an Institutional Climate to Encourage Minority Participation in Higher Education." *Peabody Journal of Education* 66 (Fall): 32-45.

Bremmer, Brian (1992) "A Spicier Stew in the Melting Pot." *Business Week* (December 21): 29.

Busch, J.W. (1985). "Mentoring in Graduate Schools of Education." *American Educational Research.* Journal 22 (Summer): 257-265.

Campbell, Jeanne L. and Michael Q. Patton (1988). *Lessons from Effective Philanthropy.* A Report to the Board of Directors of the McKnight Foundation.

Carnegie Corporation (1983). *Education and Economic Progress: Toward a National Education Policy.* New York: Carnegie Corporation.

Carrington, C.H. and Sedlacek, W.E. (1976). *Attitudes and Characteristics of Black Graduate Students.* (Report No.CSC-RR-3-76). University of Maryland, College Park: Cultural Study Center.

Carter, Deborah J. and Reginald Wilson (1989). *Eighth Annual Status Report: Minorities in Higher Education.* Washington,D.C.: American Council on Education.

Chandler, T.L. (1988). *Attracting Minority Graduate Students and Faculty in an Atmosphere of Increasing Competition.* Paper presented at an Idea Exchange Meeting of the Council of Graduate Schools, Chicago, IL.

Claque, Monique (1990). *Minority Doctoral Support Programs: Three Case Studies.* College Park, Md.: National Center for Postsecondary Governance and Finance, University of Maryland.

Clewell, B.C. (1987). *Retention of Black and Hispanic Doctoral Students*. Part I: Personal and Background Characteristics of Persisting and Nonpersisting Black and Hispanic Graduate Students. Part II: Retention of Minority Doctoral Students: Institutional Policies and Practices. (GRE Board Reearch Report No. 83-4R. ETS Research Report, 87-10, 96pp.).Princeton, NJ: Educational Testing Service.

College Board (1985). *Equality and Excellence: The Educational Status of Black Americans*. New York: College Entrance Examination Board.

Collison, M. N-K, (1987). "How Four Predominantly White Colleges Succeed in Retaining Black and Hispanic Students." *Chronicle of Higher Education*. 33(22), 31-34.

Crase, D. and Walker, H. (1987). *Black Students and Professionals in Health Education*. ERIC Document Reproduction Service No. ED 292 755).

Desegregating America's Colleges and Universities, Title VI Regulation of Higher Education. John B. Williams, III, 1988.

Epps, Edgar G. and K.W. Jackson (1988). "The Educational Attainment Process Among Black Youth." In John B. Williams III (Ed.) *Desegregating America's Colleges and Universities. New York*: Teachers College Press.

Fang, W.L., et. al. (1987, October). "Assessing Racial Attitudes in a University Setting." (10pp.). Paper presented at the Annual Meeting of the American Evaluation Association, Boston, MA.

Finn, Chester E., Jr (1987). "Raising the Stakes, How Colleges Could Really Improve the Schools." *Change* Magazine (May/ June).

Flemming, Jacqueline (1984). *Blacks in College.* San Francisco: Jossey-Bass.

Florida Education Fund (1989). *Annual Report.* Tampa, Florida: Florida Education Fund for Higher Education.

Goyer, John C. and Peter C. Pineo, (1974). "Minority Group Status and Self-Evaluated Class." *The Sociological Quarterly.* 15:199-211.

Gusfield, Joseph (1970). "Beyond Berkeley." In Howard Becker (ed.). *Campus Power Struggle.* Chicago: Trans-action Books.

Hall, M.L. and Allen, W.R. (1982). "Race Consciousness and Achievement: Two Issues in the Study of Black Graduate/ Professional Students". *Integrated Education*, 20, 56-61.

Harvey, William B. (1986). "Where Are the Black Faculty Members?" *Chronicle of Higher Education* (January 22): 96.

Heiss, Jerold and Susan Ownes. (1972). "Self-Evaulations and Blacks and Whites." *American Journal of Sociology.* 78:360-370.

Hilliard, A. (1990, October). Paper presented at the 4th Annual McKnight Fellows Meeting. Tampa, FL.

Hodgkinson, Harold L. (1985). *All One System: Demographics of Education, Kindergarten through Graduate School.* Washington, D.C.: Institute for Educational Leadership.

Horowitz, Helen L. (1986). "Why So Many Students are Grinds." *The Chronicle of Higher Education.* 31 (January 8):112.

Isaac, P.D.(1986). *Recruitment, Retention, and Graduation of Minority Graduate Students.* Paper presented at the Annual Convention of the American Psychological Association, Washington, D.C.

Kolbert, E. (1989, January 8). "The Scramble for Black Professors." *New York Times.* (32-35).

Lasch, Christopher (1978). *The Culture of Narcissism: American Life in Age of Diminishing Expectations.* New York: W.W.Norton.

Lee, V. (1985). *Access to Higher Education: The Experience of Blacks, Hispanics and Low Socio-economic Status Whites.* Washington, D.C.: American Council on Education.

Levinson, Daniel J. (1978). *The Seasons of a Man's Life.* New York: Ballantine.

Marks, J.L. (1984). *Higher Education Enrollment, 1982: Trends in the Nation and the South.* (107pp.). Atlanta, GA: Southern Regional Education Board.

McKenna, P.G. and V. Lewis (1986). Tapping Potential: Ten Steps for Retaining Underrepresented Students." *Journal of College Student Personnel.* 21 (Summer):452-453.

Mingle, J.R. (1988). *Focus on Minorities: Trends in Higher Education Participation and Success.* Denver, CO: The Education Commission of the States and the State Higher Education Executive Officers.

Minorities in the Graduate Education Pipeline, Shirley Vining Brown. 1987.

Mommsen, K.G. (1974). "Black Doctorates in American Higher Education: A Cohort Analysis." *Journal of Social and Behavioral Sciences,* 21, 101-117.

National Commission on Excellence Reform (1983). *A Nation at Risk: The Imperative for Educational Reform.* Washington, D.C.: U.S. Department of Education.

National Academy of Sciences. (1977). *Retention of Minority Students in Engineering.* A Report of the Retention Task Force, Committee on Minorities in Engineering, Assembly of Engineering, National Research Council. (113pp.).

Nettles, Michael (1988). *Toward Black Undergraduate Student Equality in Higher Education.* Westport, CT: Greenwood Press.

Nettles, Michael T. (1990). B*lack, Hispanic, and White Doctoral Students: Before, During, and After Enrolling in Graduate School.* (Research Report). Princeton, NJ: Educational Testing Service.

Owens, O.H. (1976). *A Study of Black Graduate Students in Alabama.* (102pp.). University, AL: The University Institute of Higher Education Research and Services.

Pruitt, A.S. and P.D. Issac (1985). "Discrimination in Recruitment, Admission and Retention of Minority Graduate Students." *Journal of Negro Education.* 54 (Fall):526-536.

Quality Education for Minorities Project (1990). *Education That Works: An Action Plan for the Education of Minorities.* Cambridge, Mass.: Massachusetts Institute of Technology.

Richardson, Richard C. (1989). *Institutional Climate and Minority Achievement.* Denver, Colorado: Education Commission of the States.

Richardson, Richard L. and S.C. Gerlach (1980). "Black Dropouts: A Study of Significant Factors Contributing to a Black Student's Decision." *Urban Education.* 14(January):489-494.

Ryan, P. (1989). "Blacks Suffer in a Nightmare that Many Immigrants Escape." *The Tampa Tribune.* Section 1-2A, Tuesday, July 25th.

Scott, Gloria (1981). "The Economic Future: Institutional and Student Financial Aid for Blacks in Higher Education." In Gail E. Thomas (Ed.). *Black Students in Higher Education* (pp.105-115). Dix Hill, NY: General Hall.

Seidman, Harold (1988). "The Quasi World of Federal Government." *The Brookings Review.* (Summer):23-27.

Sewell, William H., A.D. Haller and A. Portes (1970). "The Educational and Early Occupational Attainment Process: Replication and Revision." *American Sociological Review.* 35:1014-1027.

Skolnick, Jerome H. (1969). *The Politics of Protest.* New York: Ballantine Books.

Smythe, H.H. (1976). "The Black Professional." *The Black American Reference Book.* Englewood Cliffs, NJ: Prentice Hall.

State Higher Education Executive Officers (1987). *A Difference of Degrees: State Initiatives to Improve Minority Student Achievement.* Report and Recommendation of the State Higher Education Executive Officers Task Force on Minority Student Achievement. Denver, Colorado: State Higher Education Executive Officers.

Thomas, Gail E. (1987). "Black College Students and Their Major Field of Choice." In Anne S. Pruitt (Ed.). *In Pursuit of Equality in Higher Education* (pp.105-115). Dix Hills, NY: General Hall.

Treisman, Philip Uri (1986). *Improving the Performance of Minority Students in College-Level Mathematics.*

Trent, William and Elaine Copeland (1988). "The Production of Black Doctoral Recipients: A Description of Five States' Progress." In John Williams (Ed.). *Desegregating America's Colleges and Universities: Title VI Regulation of Higher Education.* (pp.54-70). New York: Teachers Colleges Press.

Tribble, Israel (1988). "Attracting African Americans and Other Disadvantaged Minorities into Mainstream Faculty Careers: Lessons From the Florida Education Fund." Unpublished paper presented at the March 1988 National Conference of Higher Education.

Upton, James and Anne E. Pruitt (1985). *Financial Assistance to Black Doctoral Students in Two Adams' States: A Policy Analysis.* Atlanta, GA: Southern Education Foundation.

VANT and Associates (1988). *A Study of the Factors Influencing Blacks Going on to Graduate and Professional Schools.* Tampa, FL: State Board of Education Advisory Committee on the Education of Blacks in Florida.

Weber, Max (1952). "The Essentials of Bureaucratic Organization: An Ideal-Type Construction." In Robert K. Merton, Ailsa P.Gray, Barbara Hockey and Hanan C. Selvin (eds.) *Reader in Bureaucracy.* New York: The Free Press.

Willie, Charles V. and Arline McCord (1972). *Black Students at White Colleges.* New York: Praeger.

Willie, Charles V. and Donald Cunnigen (1981). "Black Students in Higher Education." *Annual Review of Sociology.* 7:117-98.

Willie, Charles V. (1987). *Effective Education.* Westport, CT: Greenwood Press.

Willie, V., Michael K. Grady and Richard O. Hope (1991). *African-Americans and the Doctoral Experiences: Implications for Policy.* New York: Teachers College, Columbia University.

Wilson, Reginald and Manuel J. Justiz (1987-88). "Minorities in Higher Education: Confronting a Time Bomb." *Educational Record* (Fall-Winter):9-14.

Wolfe, Tom (1976). "The Me Decade and the Third Great Awakening." *New Yorker.* 23(August).

Wycliff, Don (1990). "Blacks' Advance Slow in Science Careers." *The New York Times.* (June 8):A1 and A9.